Shaking the Skies

Dedicated to

The men and women of the aviation industry who made the global village a reality, providing the safest mode of transportation.

The great IATA team who worked with me with passion, speed and commitment to turn my impossible targets into a tangible reality.

GOLD MERCURY
INTERNATIONAL

Shaking
the Skies

The untold story of aviation since 9/11 and the
biggest turnaround of an international organization
in history – by the man who managed $2.5 trillion
and made aviation greener and safer.

GIOVANNI BISIGNANI

Former Director General and CEO of the
International Air Transport Association

LONDON   MADRID
NEW YORK   MEXICO CITY
BOGOTA   BUENOS AIRES
BARCELONA   MONTERREY

Published by
LID Publishing Ltd.
6-8 Underwood Street
London N1 7JQ (United Kingdom)
info@lidpublishing.com
LIDPUBLISHING.COM

A member of:

www.businesspublishersroundtable.com

© Giovanni Bisignani
© LID Publishing Ltd. 2013

Reprinted twice 2013

Printed and bound in Great Britain by CPI Group (UK) Ltd, Croydon, CR0 4YY

ISBN: 978-1-907794-36-0
ISBN: 978-1-907794-54-4 (Airport Edition)

Design: e-Digital Design Ltd

CONTENTS

Chapter Six: THE FUTURE IS GREEN

Environmental initiatives, including airspace issues and the EU ETS

Chapter Seven: SAFETY FIRST

Making the skies ever safer

Chapter Eight: BAD PEOPLE, NOT BAD OBJECTS

The need for more efficient and harmonized security

Chapter Nine: VISION 2050
A look at Vision 2050, liberalization
and thoughts on the future

PROLOGUE

The day that changed the world

There are two aviation-related events that we will never forget. We all remember where we were, who we were with and what was said.

The first occurred on 20 July 1969. When Neil Armstrong told Houston "The Eagle has landed", we all held our breath, captivated by the courage, the technological genius, and the sheer scale of the achievement. Neil followed this with one of the most famous remarks in history—"one small step for man, one giant leap for mankind"—and it seemed as if, as one, the entire world looked up at the sky and tried to see him taking that giant leap on behalf of us all, jumping down the ladder onto the surface of the moon.

On that day, we all dreamed about the power of flight to do good and unite the world.

The second event forever imprinted on our minds is 9/11. This cowardly terrorist attack on civilians is remembered for all the wrong reasons—for the destruction, the loss of life and that terrible feeling we all had that the world had changed forever.

At 8:45am, American Airlines Flight 11, travelling from Boston to Los Angeles, smashed into the North Tower of the World Trade Center in New York. United Airlines Flight 175 hit the South Tower just minutes later. A third plane hit the Pentagon and a fourth crashed in rural Pennsylvania.

United States airspace was closed at 9:21am, the first time this had happened in Federal Aviation Administration (FAA) history. All commercial flights were grounded and an hour later Vice President Dick Cheney issued orders to shoot down any commercial aircraft that was suspected of being hijacked.

On that tragic Tuesday, nearly 3,000 people lost their lives.

The knock-on effects were huge. The world economy was deeply affected and the New York Stock Exchange had to close for a week. Air travel dipped alarmingly too. And we're still paying the price in terms of intrusive, uncoordinated and lengthy security measures.

It was hard to believe that aviation had been used as a weapon to strike divisions in the global village that it had made a reality. Airlines connect economies, cultures and families. That they were used to destroy these things is still very painful for all of us involved in aviation.

Despite the significance of the events, when they happened I never imagined that they would have such an effect on my personal life and my professional career as they did.

Some 20 years after he became the first man on the moon, I had the pleasure of meeting Neil Armstrong. He became a very special friend and we met every year with other aviation colleagues at a wonderful ranch in Wyoming. I have vivid recollections of Neil entertaining us with fascinating stories as we sat by a large, round fireplace. But it was Neil's friendship that really provided the warmth as he recounted his many adventures, always as if it was just normal, routine business and always finishing with a knowing smile.

While the moon landing was significant on a personal level, 9/11 affected me professionally. On that fateful day, I was in my office in London preparing for the launch of the online travel agency, OPODO. The launch was just over a month away and as CEO I had a lot of work to do. But a colleague burst into my office and told me of a frantic phone call from New York. We went quickly to the Boardroom and watched the terrible event unfold on the TV.

Just over a month later there was another phone call from New York. This time, it was Leo Mullin, CEO of Delta Air Lines and also Chairman of the Board for the International Air Transport Association (IATA). He invited me to New York to meet him. At that meeting he offered me the job of Director General and CEO of IATA. He said he needed me to make the Association relevant and help turnaround the industry from the terrible, dark days of 9/11.

"You will have a blank sheet of paper, a licence to change everything," he said. "We need you to lead a revolution."

CHAPTER ONE
Why Me?

Background and arrival at IATA

A change of heart

This is a book about change, about its challenges and the talents necessary to drive it through. Specifically, it is about changing the world's most important and event-shaping industry—aviation. Some of these changes will have been noticed by the passenger while others concentrated on back-end industry processes. For every change, flying has become safer, easier and a lot more enjoyable.

It's as well to start with perhaps the greatest change of all, the one that starts the ball rolling. Although I had never given a categorical "no" when asked if I was interested in the role of Director General and CEO of the International Air Transport Association (IATA), I had not jumped at the chance either. It was 2001 and I was in a good place, literally and figuratively. Besides, I wasn't convinced I would be given the tools needed to do the IATA job properly, nor was I sure the association was ready to accept a radical change in the way it was run.

IATA was old-school and proud to be so. The bigger, established carriers dominated proceedings. Change was not in IATA's vocabulary and rather than help shape world and industry events, it seemed paralyzed by them. After 9/11, the best it could offer was a "no unnecessary flights" instruction to its own staff.

But that was also what made it a great challenge, one that would require every skill I had acquired in my career to date. And I love challenges. Leo Mullin, IATA Chairman and CEO of Delta Air Lines, called me again just before Christmas 2001 to insist that the IATA Board would empower me to make the changes required. Jürgen Weber, the Lufthansa CEO and an IATA Board member, echoed the sentiment. "Push," he said, "and others will follow."

I was persuaded by these kind words of encouragement. So I changed my mind, went to meet Leo in New York, and accepted the job.

Walking into a collapsing structure

IATA is the industry association for most of the world's airlines. In plain figures, it represents approximately 240 carriers and 84% of the world's scheduled air traffic. Some 80 IATA offices around the world help to administer processes integral to the running of the industry—from a $300 billion-plus per year financial clearing house to an audit on safety practices.

Overall, aviation supports more than 56 million jobs and generates around $2.2 trillion in global revenues. These figures don't include tourism or other jobs made possible by air travel. Nor do they include domestic trade and tourism. In short, there isn't a person on the planet that isn't affected in some way, shape or form by aviation. If you want to visit family living overseas or simply need a vacation to soak up the sun or the peculiarities of a different culture—even if you want strawberries out of season—airlines make it all possible.

Such facts suggest running an airline is a good business to be in. Well, it is a *great* business to be in—unless you want to make money. Airlines have never come close to returning the cost of capital, averaging less than 1% profit over the last 60 years. Not coincidentally, it was about 60 years ago that the rules of the modern industry were framed. Despite globalization, the jet engine, the Internet, low-cost carriers and a million and one other developments, these antiquated rules are still in place. Airlines may fly like a bird but they are certainly not as free as one. Too many governments have yet to recognize that a national flag on the tail has lost its significance. Having a national airline is a hobby many of them can no longer afford. Meanwhile, the politicians in developed nations view aviation as a convenient cash cow. They are diligent in imposing taxes, negligent in dealing with monopolies. It has led to the most extraordinary value chain where the principal component—the airline—is the only part that doesn't rejoice in double-digit returns.

When a world-shattering event like 9/11 gets dumped on top of this wobbly framework, it should come as no surprise that the industry was on the verge of collapse by early 2002. The 1990s had been relatively good years, culminating in a 1999 profit of around $8 billion. But that proved to be the peak of airline performance. From 2001–05, the industry lost around $40 billion. Over half of that total disappeared in 2001 and 2002. Stalwarts of the industry such as Swissair, Air Afrique, Ansett, Sabena and TWA were no more. By 2003, with Severe Acute Respiratory Syndrome (SARS), the war in Iraq and a global economic downturn further eroding industry foundations, the top six US airlines were $100 billion in debt with a market capitalization of just $4 billion. A third of Latin America carriers were technically bankrupt.

My time at IATA brought me up against each of these harsh truths and many more besides. But it was also an opportunity, a chance for IATA to blow away the cobwebs and lead the industry toward sustainability. I knew that if air transport was to continue its role as a catalyst for world development, it needed to change—quickly and dramatically.

Leading a revolution

Initially I was cool on the IATA position because I really was very happy in my existing role and location. I was heading up the online travel company OPODO from offices in Covent Garden in London.

OPODO was the first time in my career I had the opportunity to start something from scratch. My task was to make the company the number one online travel agent in Europe. It was a well-backed operation, established by three giants of European aviation: Lufthansa, Air France and British Airways. CEOs Jürgen Weber, Jean-Cyril Spinetta and Rod Eddington—the most visionary European leaders at that time—had invested some $300 million in the project.

Distribution—how and where an airline sells its tickets to the customer—was undergoing a revolution thanks to the Internet and I was delighted to be given the opportunity to develop this new sales channel. I wasn't a complete novice in the dark art of distribution even if the Internet was then, and remains still, a minefield. In the 1990s, I was the Chairman of Galileo, a Global Distribution System (GDS), which basically allows travel agents to sell airline tickets, and I was the driver of the very successful Galileo/COVIA merger. Successful for the companies concerned that is. Successful from an airline point of view? Not exactly.

Galileo and COVIA were typical examples of the air transport industry developing cutting-edge ideas but lacking sufficient resources to progress them into a real-world business situation. They end up selling these new tools to developers and then scratching around for enough crumbs to pay the exorbitant fees being demanded of them to use the very ideas they created.

Galileo and COVIA mirrored each other, one operating in Europe, one in the United States. For me, with a Harvard business background and a fresh point of view, it made no sense to exist in parallel dimensions. A merger was frowned upon initially, especially as COVIA looked to be the dominant partner. My good friend, Otto Loepfe, then CEO of Swissair, was quite upset that an Italian was pushing for the tie-up. "Why would you want to kill a company that bears the name of such a famous countryman?" he asked. Fortunately, there was an easy solution that prevented me from supposedly betraying my country. We kept the Galileo name but moved its operations into the COVIA structure so the company accrued maximum benefit from the merger.

I had moved on to OPODO by the time 9/11 hit. We watched speechless in our offices as the second plane hit the South Tower. I knew this event was industry-changing, world-changing even, but I had no idea that it would also alter the course of my career. In the immediate aftermath of the tragedy we moved rapidly to reconfigure OPODO, although I insisted on staying true to the planned November launch. We laid off some staff and reduced costs but the project remained a priority for the airline owners.

Around this time I met up with Jeff Katz, founder of Orbitz, the precursor of OPODO in the United States. He gave me some good advice and it only cost me a couple of dinners. I'll say more about the value of personal relationships in business but for now let's just say that two expensive meals can sometimes work out to be a cheap deal. In contrast, management consultants McKinsey, hired by the shareholders to build a business plan, put in a rather more flamboyant multi-million dollar bill. I didn't even get dinner out of it.

McKinsey's final report did make some interesting points in its marketing analysis though. OPODO should not use the logos of the airline founders in their home markets as the brands were associated with high cost there. The suggestion was to use only the IATA logo, since OPODO was an accredited agent and consumers equated IATA with reliability—even if it was somewhat dusty and outdated and very few knew what the association actually represented. It was a bit embarrassing explaining this to the airline shareholders who were so used to promoting their brands. I knew I was asking the airlines to make a big concession. But I agreed with McKinsey and successfully fought our corner.

Because OPODO was a trailblazing project, I had to face intense media scrutiny. Richard Quest of CNN, previously with the BBC, was the first one to put me on the spot. Just a week before launch he faced me squarely, live on CNN Prime Time, and told me that OPODO would never get approval from the Competition Commission. It was airlines colluding with OPODO, he said, and giving away preferential fares to the Internet company they owned. Something simple to start the media campaign then! I was delighted to fend off Richard fairly and squarely—OPODO was competing on a level playing field and had the best fares because we had the best website and the most efficient distribution model. I was even able to show that airlines other than the three owners were giving us their best fares. They saw OPODO as a very innovative and effective portal and this was driving the business. The story died a death and shortly after I met Mario Monti, the European Commission's Vice President in Brussels, who was happy to give OPODO competition clearance.

OPODO launched on time and within a couple of months it had grown to be the most visited travel site in both the United Kingdom and Germany. I felt like we had reached the summit of a mountain. In reality, although I didn't know it, I was already standing at the bottom of another one.

In November 2001, as we were launching OPODO in the German market, I got a call out of the blue to go to New York and meet with Leo Mullin. I didn't know Leo personally but knew he was CEO of Delta Air Lines so automatically assumed he wanted to talk about a possible tie-up with Orbitz, Delta being a stakeholder in the US company. The idea had already been mooted with Jeff Katz but it was on the back-burner until OPODO matured.

Aviation recruitment specialist Michael Bell, of Spencer Stuart, soon put me straight. The meeting was about IATA. As a former CEO of Alitalia and an IATA Board member I was well-versed in the lore of the association. Pierre Jeanniot, then IATA Director General, was an old acquaintance and I had attended the 2000 IATA AGM in Madrid at his invitation. But I couldn't imagine why they would want to headhunt me. I'm not a neutral man, a fence-sitter. In my business experience, I was always fighting for or against something. IATA by contrast had found the fence very comfortable. Michael revealed that the search for Pierre's successor had been going on for a while but had stepped up a gear after 9/11. It had become the Board's urgent priority.

I accepted the invitation to meet Leo mainly out of curiosity. We met in Spencer Stuart's Park Avenue offices and immediately built up a good rapport. Leo was stressing urgency in the new DG appointment as a proposal had to be presented to the IATA Board the following month.

We reviewed my work experience, not just as head of OPODO but also my time leading Alitalia and my international experience with Italian conglomerate IRI—one of the largest corporations in the world with 500,000 employees and $50 billion in revenues. As Head of the International Division, I was personally responsible for a significant percentage of that. My IRI role brought me into contact with different cultures and government decision-makers, including many Presidents and Prime Ministers. This obviously struck a chord with Leo who understood that high-level political support and negotiation experience was essential if IATA's traditional approach was to change.

Taking Leo through my personal history it was becoming increasingly obvious that my background did indeed match IATA's needs. But I was a long way from being convinced that the job was right for me. At the 2000 AGM I was struck by how little IATA had changed since my Board member days during the early 1990s. Ten years and a huge change in market dynamics, including 9/11, had failed to budge IATA from its comfortable perch. I couldn't imagine having to oversee another ten years of solid indifference while the world wobbled in geopolitical and economic turbulence.

Decision time

Advice doesn't come any better than from Jack Welch, my mentor, business hero and, I am happy to say, a personal friend. I've known the legendary businessman since the 1980s and we often spend time together socially with our wives. I recall in particular a wonderful week in Palm Beach when Jack introduced my wife and me to golf. Traditionally, we spent a week in Capri and followed this by watching the French Open tennis at Roland Garros, Paris.

I told Jack about my meeting with Leo and, since we were both in New York, we arranged to have lunch at a trendy, well-known restaurant. Talking with Jack wasn't easy. It's not that he isn't a great conversationalist but he had just released his latest book, *Straight from the Gut*, and was signing autographs like a rock star. We had to slot in our conversation between adoring visits from business groupies. I told Jack about my impression of IATA—a dusty cave, dark and full of creatures afraid of the light of day. Jack shrugged and said without hesitation to jump on board. The situation was critical and in his opinion that made it a great time to join.

More meetings followed. First, Xavier de Irala, head of Iberia, in Madrid and then Isao Kaneko, CEO of Japan Airlines, in London. Kaneko was very persuasive about the need for change. Although I didn't know it at the time, he was about to get very busy with the merger with Japan Air Systems. Unfortunately, Kaneko hit a very real problem with consolidation, which is how to keep pilots happy. The issue is seniority and pay levels, underlined by some very strong unions. But more often than not, pilots will claim any disagreement is about safety. It is rarely the truth. The Japanese Minister responsible listened to the unions, however, and although Kaneko was able to chair the IATA AGM in Tokyo in 2005, he left JAL the day after the AGM finished.

Both Irala and Kaneko were members of the IATA Board of Governors and both insisted that the Board was pushing for real and tangible change. It was Leo Mullin and Jürgen Weber who finally persuaded me to join IATA, although to be honest the real decision-maker was my wife Elena. She wasn't keen at first, wary of what she thought would be constant trips between IATA's main offices in Geneva and Montreal. We also worried that I wouldn't have much time to spend with our daughter, Claudia, who lives and works in Rome. But both Elena and Claudia eventually saw the challenge as too big to refuse. It was a good job Elena didn't know I would be away for 20 days a month otherwise we would never have got past the first phone call. In return for her support, I promised her that I would stop working at 65 and we would return to live in London. As a gesture of intent we bought an apartment a couple of blocks away from where we were living during my OPODO days.

Decision made, I asked Leo exactly what he wanted from me. "IATA is a reliable association," he said, "but it is no longer relevant to the industry."

The word relevant started to buzz in my mind. Understanding what that meant in the context of IATA wasn't easy. IATA is an association, not a straightforward commercial business. It started life in 1945 when just about every airline was state-owned. IATA doesn't have competitors in the typical sense, it isn't listed on the stock market and it is a Canadian not-for-profit corporation.

This was my first clue. Somehow, IATA had come to translate its brief as a "not-for-making-money" organization, a "not-for-change" organization or a "not-to-be-run-like-a-business" organization. But if we were to serve our members properly we needed to be efficient, anticipate their requirements and realize enough money from commercial operations to assist any members in need. Most of all, we needed to provide leadership by building a consensus among all our members and not just a happy few. I knew that IATA was a big boys club, ruled by the major airlines. I also knew that suggesting consensus—seeking the support and understanding the needs of smaller carriers from emerging regions—would raise a few eyebrows.

But 9/11 had changed the rules of the game. The industry was collapsing and airlines were going out of business left, right and centre. Through IATA I had a once-in-a-lifetime opportunity to reshape the industry.

Assessing the situation

Any leader has to make an honest assessment of the challenges ahead and the ones being left behind. I found leaving OPODO very difficult. It was my baby, a start-up company that introduced an innovative distribution model to the industry. After months of 12-hour-plus days we were beginning to enjoy a lot of deserved success. I was baling out just as the good times were beginning to roll.

And yes, the challenge at IATA was immense and very tempting but the crisis was unprecedented and the major airlines held all the cards. What was good for the big guys was good for the industry, or so they thought.

On top of this, IATA was in an acute financial situation. There was a couple of months' worth of cash, no assets and there was a $30-million mortgage on our headquarters. Most of IATA's money came from members' dues and fees for service. Agreeing the funding for a new project was a long and painful process because it inevitably meant asking members for more cash. That lost the association its flexibility. New projects were old and obsolete by the time they got approval, let alone delivered.

My friend and former IATA DG, Pierre Jeanniot, had done well to bring the industry settlement systems—the back-end process that ensured airlines got their money from travel agents and other stakeholders—into the IATA fold in the 1990s. That was no easy task. But apart from that, there was not even a whisper of change. Would I really get Board support for a revolution?

Maybe. More of a certainty was that getting any kind of support from the majority of the IATA management team would be a pipedream. Many of them had ended up at the association having failed to gain a promotion at an airline. IATA was the pre-retirement destination of choice, a sort of winding down halfway house between business and leisure. Others had a government background, which gave them the same sense of urgency as a United Nations study group. They wouldn't cut it in the real world of competitive business.

To my knowledge, nobody at IATA had ever been fired. And the most ferocious yearly target was "how many meetings have you had with a member airline in the last 12 months?" This was a clear indication of the malaise in IATA management. I bet whomever looked after Air Seychelles was a star performer.

In short, IATA knew little about getting results as measured by exacting business targets. It was an institution doing what it had always done.

The right man

Understanding the challenges is only one part of the equation. Another is understanding yourself. What would I bring to the job? Looking back over my life and career, it was apparent that managing change had been a constant factor.

My schooling began in Milan in the 1950s but the family soon moved to Buenos Aires as my father had become CEO of Pirelli Argentina. We stayed there for nine important, formative years. I have retained a great love of the Spanish language and Latin American culture, and clearly my time there invested me with a spirit of multiculturalism. Returning to Italy I graduated from La Sapienza, the University of Rome, and became Assistant Professor at the Economics and Commerce School there. The sudden death of my father in 1970 prompted me to move on, this time to New York where I got a job with the First National City Bank. Coincidentally, the office was on Park Avenue, a couple of blocks away from where I met Leo, and every day I walked past the then famous Pan Am building. Pan Am is no more and their headquarters is now called the MetLife building, which provides a quick snapshot of how well airlines have fared over the years.

Moving to the United States was not just about experiencing another culture. I also added some important skills. I was working with the bank's International Division and was part of a small team that invented and launched the first Eurodollar loans, which focus on US deposits in foreign banks. I got used to handling large sums of money and a different way of working. The American and European work environments were poles apart at the time. The US experience taught me to handle pressure, respond to tough targets and deliver with speed.

I moved on to study at Harvard Business School with Professor Roland Christensen. My work there gave me a great foundation in understanding how to change a business. The book my research project was based on, Arthur Chandler's *Strategy and Structure*, became a business bible for me and I've often referred back to it throughout my career.

After finishing at Harvard, I went back to Italy and in 1976 started work for ENI, a major oil company. I was the Chief of Staff for the CEO, Pietro Sette. Previously, Sette had been the lawyer and advisor for the founder of ENI, Enrico Mattei. As such, Sette was instrumental in devising the famous 50/50 profit sharing deal with Middle East oil producers. It was a deal that revolutionized the oil business. Tragically, Enrico Mattei was killed when the company aircraft crashed in mysterious circumstances; most probably because of a bomb. Sette eventually became CEO of ENI and I became his closest aid.

I had a significant role in top-level meetings and discussions, particularly in Africa, the Middle East and the Far East, because Sette didn't speak English particularly well. Every meeting was planned thoroughly. Our policy was to first build up a personal relationship so we knew exactly who we were talking to, their likes and dislikes. The business proposition was only mentioned once a level of trust and communication had been established. Sette was a sophisticated negotiator and a great mentor. He understood that even in business, having the right arguments was only half the battle. You also have to elicit the right feelings. You must be somebody with whom your counterpart *wants* to do business—not just somebody with whom they *should* do business.

We operated at the highest level. For example, I had the dubious pleasure of meeting Colonel Gadaffi when ENI was drilling in international waters between Tunisia and Libya. He was arrogant and unpleasant and there was a very tense atmosphere because he wanted to unilaterally extend Libyan waters to gain control of an important oil platform. I remember this well because I met him again when I became IATA Director General and he was a completely different man, very softly spoken and genuinely interested in the discussion. Gaddafi believed a new Libyan airline would be a useful tool to help his country extend its influence abroad. He needed IATA support in building the right infrastructure. Afriqiyah Airways was born and stepped into the gap left by Air Afrique and the French airline, UTA. The only awkward point came when Gaddafi asked me what I liked most about Libya. I said I had only had the opportunity to stay for a night at a time so couldn't really comment. When he pressed, I mentioned that I really liked the dates that were available from the local markets. On my way to the airport, complete with police escort, the driver suddenly stopped at the local market. Clearly the intention was to buy some dates for me but the noise and confusion caused by the police suddenly stopping scared off the stallholders and I had to leave the country empty handed. A week or so later, I received a big box of fresh dates complete with a very polite note from Gaddafi.

I was also involved in negotiations with an Algerian company, Sonatrach, that set up the first trans-Mediterranean gas pipe from Algeria to Northern Italy. Their Chairman, Sid Ahmed Ghozali, later became President of his country and I enjoyed a good relationship with him for many years. We used to go jogging together at 6am when he was in Rome, enjoying the peace and quiet of the Villa Borghese park but tracked all the way by a very conspicuous police force.

After a few years at ENI, I made another change. Sette had moved to IRI, a holding company for some 500 firms and $50 billion in revenues. It included many famous Italian brands under its umbrella, such as Alfa Romeo, Aeritalia, Alitalia and most of the Italian banks. The company was set up by Mussolini after the 1929 Wall Street crisis to bolster Italian industry and it also played a leading role in rebuilding Italy after the Second World War. I followed my boss, initially in the same Chief of Staff position. I later became Senior Vice President of International Affairs, responsible for IRI's international strategy and around $10 billion in revenues. The role gave me the opportunity to further my contacts at the highest level.

In India, after I had negotiated the sale of petrochemical refineries and power generation plants, Sette and I explained the benefits of the deal to Indira Gandhi. We had tea together on many occasions in the most beautiful gardens imaginable, part of her official residence in New Delhi. It was in these gardens that she was later assassinated by two of her bodyguards, who shot her 31 times. She was a strong lady and talked passionately about India and its role in the world. Her two sons were on very different paths at that time. The younger son, Sanjay, had been the chosen heir but died in a flying accident in 1980. The elder son, Rajiv, was a pilot at Air India but was persuaded by his mother to be her political successor. Rajiv was a kind, friendly man, and it amazed me he could be so personable and yet slip seamlessly into the role of leader of the largest democracy in the world. I carried on meeting with him even after he became Prime Minister and established a good personal relationship. Rajiv loved Alfa Romeo cars. He knew all the latest developments, the nuances of each model. Fortunately, I did my homework and we always had a lively exchange on the car manufacturer's future as well as aviation issues.

While at IRI, I also got to meet someone who has since become a close friend. Singapore's Prime Minister Lee Kuan Yew became involved with IRI when we were trying to find a good location to expand SGS

Microelectronica into the semiconductor wafer fabrication process. Meeting him was a truly enriching experience. He had an unbelievable vision for Singapore even though seemingly insurmountable obstacles lay ahead. He proved that a clear strategy and determined leadership can see you through any challenge. Even now, over 80 years old, he still looks to the future. His vision and leadership have always been an inspiration to me and what he has achieved should always be held up as an example for aviation to follow.

In 2003, after I had become the IATA DG, I went to see him in Singapore and presented him with an old map of Singapore Changi Airport. He had been personally involved in Changi's development and the map depicted a design he had approved. I asked him whether the airport or the airline—in which he had also played a crucial role—was more important to Singapore. He plumped for the airport but resisted dwelling on the past and instead started talking about what to do about low-cost carriers, a particular problem at the time.

While I was at IRI during the 1980s, betting on China's development seemed a reasonable wager. Plenty of the top management at IRI favoured Russia but my instinct for change told me it was going to happen fastest in this most traditional of societies. We were trying to sell China a factory for the production of seamless steel pipes for the gas industry. Together with Romano Prodi, Pietro Sette's successor as CEO, I met with Prime Minister Li Peng several times, in Rome and in Beijing. It took about three years— China wasn't yet developing at the speed for which it is currently famous— but eventually we secured a $3-billion deal. That contract was about team work. Prodi kept in contact with the Prime Minister while I worked with the Mayor of Tianjin, Li Ruihuan, on details. Li Ruihuan was on his way to becoming a very influential figure in Chinese politics and persuading them both pushed the contract through. We built a plant in Tianjin, in the Northeast of the country. In those days driving from Beijing to Tianjin was a difficult, tiring journey taking several hours. But as evidence we made the right decision in investing in China, the journey can now be made in around 30 minutes on the Jingjintang Highway. Relations with the Chinese leadership remained strong throughout my time with IRI and I developed further deals in other sectors, such as telecoms.

I think the main reason I developed so many good relationships with world leaders while I was at IRI—apart from thorough homework—was that I never bored them with politics. Thankfully, that meant they never bored me with politics either. We simply talked about business cooperation and I think that was a great relief for them. It certainly was for me.

What all this really taught me was that there is always common ground. Prepare well, find that common ground and build up the relationship. And once that link is formed, work hard to maintain it, no matter how the business deal develops. Personal contacts are the lifeblood of business.

Alitalia

My good work at IRI got me my first CEO-level job at Alitalia in 1989. I was instantly grateful for the negotiation skills I had acquired because the airline was on the verge of imploding. It was plagued with strikes, there were constant confrontations both internal and external, and the route structure ensured profitability was a distant prospect.

Alitalia had 86% of the Italian market at the time and controlled all the airports with the exception of Malpensa in Milan, which was owned by the City. My appointment got strong support from the shareholders and trade unions. I had a mandate to change everything. This was just as well because everything needed changing.

I began by studying the balance sheet and meeting with all the management. Renegotiating the union contracts was a must. I managed to win the unions over by ceding some salary increases but gaining an awful lot more in efficiency. It was a win–win deal because it boosted morale as well as services and we were soon in a positive recovery phase. That helped convince my shareholder, IRI, to make a massive investment in the airline and we ordered 40 Airbus A320s with CFM engines. We also got ten MD11s with GE engines and this boost to capacity further increased the upward swing of the company.

But then, having been promised the money for these purchases by my shareholders, I was told that no further capital was available. Alitalia had made a massive investment and we had to take the hit directly on our balance sheet.

New beginnings in Latin America

My time as CEO of Alitalia was very exciting. There was always a deal in the offing, a challenge to overcome. I never had a quiet day at the office. At one point, the opportunity to become involved in the privatization process of Aerolíneas Argentinas presented itself. Having spent a large part of my early years in Argentina, I have always been interested in the airline. I flew on the airline many times as a young passenger, travelling between Italy and Argentina with my parents.

So I was immediately drawn to the project. To help structure any deal, Alitalia became involved with Citibank (the new name for my former employers, the First National City Bank) and in particular with John Reed, the legendary CEO who had led the bank through a major reorganization and who later became Chairman of the New York City Stock Exchange. John was interested in the deal as he had also been raised in Argentina for a time and aviation was a sector that always captured his attention.

Alitalia was one of the leading European airlines and I felt I was in a good position at the negotiations. I knew the country well and spoke the language. I also knew the President, Carlos Menem. Years earlier, when I was working with IRI, I had invited him to lunch in Rome. At the time, he was Governor of La Rioja, a northern province in Argentina, and clearly had a bright future in front of him. His parents were from modern-day Syria but he had embraced the culture of the day and sported long hair and bushy sideburns. My Chairman, Romano Prodi, was shocked by Menem's appearance and even more shocked when I told him afterwards that he was someone to watch, a potential future President of Argentina.

I maintained good relations with Carlos Menem and in 1989 I was not at all surprised that he made my prediction come true, campaigning as a real maverick and defeating Raul Alfonsin to become President of Argentina.

Despite this personal touch, the meetings on the Aerolíneas Argentinas deal didn't go as planned. I was explaining that we had to build for the future and not just organize a rescue package for the current troubles that the airline was experiencing. But it was hard to make headway, mainly because the Argentinean government was insisting that it kept a significant portion of the shares in national hands. We couldn't see any value in the deal under those circumstances and I told my colleagues that I would try to find the right moment to explain to President Menem that we would withdraw from the deal.

I wasn't looking forward to doing that. The President believed we would find a solution and had expressed his appreciation that Alitalia and Citibank would soon be driving the Argentinean airline forward.

When you have to deliver bad news, it is best to do it face-to-face. But prepare well, including getting the timing and location of the meeting correct. It was now 1990 and the soccer World Cup was about to start. The opening match was between Argentina, the holders of the trophy, and Cameroon. The match was taking place in Milan and President Menem was in the country. I suggested a meeting in Milan as I knew he would go the game and it was better if we met away from his office. President Menem accepted my proposal and invited me to a private dinner after the match. Though my colleagues were pleased, I was concerned. I thought it best to meet for breakfast before the match. It proved to be a good decision because there was a major shock and Argentina lost to Cameroon. Having to tell President Menem that the deal was off after his team had lost a soccer match (a very serious business in Argentina) would surely have made the meeting more difficult.

At the breakfast meeting in his suite at the Principe di Savoia hotel, President Menem was in a good mood. He had had a very pleasant time the day before visiting the Ferrari headquarters. He told me that he really wanted Alitalia to win the bid for the privatization process but that other airlines were also interested. I knew this and told him that as a "porteño" (raised in Buenos Aires), I felt obliged to point him in the right direction. I knew American Airlines and SAS would not go through with the deal and said that Alitalia would regretfully also have to step out of the negotiations. Iberia was now the only possible option.

I knew the deal had no economic value because we had been exploring the options for months but, with the support of the Spanish government, Iberia went ahead and bought Aerolíneas Argentinas. Unfortunately, the CEO, Narciso Andreu—a friend of mine since my New York days—only lasted six months after the completion of the deal and the airline went back into deep red.

A very special passenger

My role as CEO also brought me into regular contact with Pope John Paul II. Although a Catholic, I don't always attend church. But the Pope was an inspiring man. Of course, his background was in heavy industry in Poland but whenever he took an Alitalia flight he never failed to have a short conversation with the *Direttore* before boarding the plane. He called me *Direttore* because a head of a company in a communist regime always has this title, and his roots in a Poland dominated by the old USSR were never far from the surface.

Planes were specially prepared for him. If it was a transatlantic flight the upper deck of a Boeing 747 would have a bed fitted. On European flights, the first five rows were cleared for the Pope and his close assistants. A section behind was reserved for Cardinals and other officials while the back of the plane held the journalists.

I often travelled with him on an Alitalia flight. On a journey from Rome to Malta I was telling the Pope about the troubles facing the airline industry and the important role Alitalia played in stimulating the national and global economy. "We are trying everything to turn the company around," I continued, "but a special blessing for the industry from the Pope would be very much appreciated at this difficult time." After a couple of weeks his personal Assistant, Monsignor Stanislaw, gave me the great news that he had decided to accept the request. We organized a big event at the Alitalia hangar at Rome's Fiumicino Airport and invited all the previous CEOs and Chairmen of all the airlines that had flown the Pope, together with any crew. Some 70 airlines were represented. The Mass and the industry Blessing were arranged for 10 December, a feast day for one of the saints that watches over aviation and by chance my birthday. It was a touching ceremony and we all felt a lot more optimistic as a result of the blessing.

The Pope always travelled with Alitalia flying out of Italy and usually returned with the national carrier of the country he was visiting. Alitalia assisted the other carriers by detailing the Pope's requirements. There was a degree of economic sense to the Pope's travel arrangements from Alitalia's point of view. Although the Pope travelled free of charge in a specially-arranged first class, the Vatican staff and journalists paid a discounted fare. Once you added up all the costs, we could just about break even.

One day, the Vatican informed Alitalia that another airline had offered to fly the Pope and all passengers free of charge. Fortunately, it was an issue easily resolved. I got Alitalia PR to mock up a TV ad, which we told Vatican staff would make up for losing the Pope's business. We had some footage of the Pope praising Alitalia, which was used internally for our staff. But we made this into a commercial and added the tagline: "Just ask a frequent flyer". The Vatican staff were surprised at first but then burst out laughing. They knew I would never have used this ad in public. We shook hands and were later honoured to learn Alitalia would continue to be the Vatican State flag carrier.

A future saint in my office

John Paul II was beatified in 2011. He is not the only one who has earned the title "Blessed" that I had to deal with during my Alitalia days. It is one of the great perks of a CEO job that you get to meet people you would never have expected to meet.

One morning, I had arrived at the office early to prepare for a budget meeting when a phone call came though from the Italian Prime Minister, Giulio Andreotti. I think he was calling from a car phone, which in those days weren't very clear, because I could hardly hear him. I gathered he was talking about an afternoon meeting with a "Ms Teresa" and so I shouted my acceptance. I didn't think much of it and passed the morning in the budget meeting. At some point in the afternoon I noticed my PA being called to reception to welcome some guests. I was expecting a business woman but instead Mother Teresa walks into my office with her young assistant. She was about 80 years old at the time but she didn't lack energy. And she was very direct with it, almost intimidating. I was busy welcoming her and paying my respects when she stopped me with a very firm gesture. "I need two worldwide passes from Alitalia," she said. "One for me, one for my assistant."

I was stunned but managed to reply that airlines usually only extend these passes to CEOs of other airlines, a courtesy and a tradition in the industry. The look in her eyes told me that was not what she wanted to hear so I quickly added that while I couldn't offer worldwide passes I could perhaps solve her problem by providing tickets any time she was flying to an Alitalia destination. She accepted this and used our services to India on a regular basis. She sent me a kind card of appreciation and I thought that was the end of the matter.

Several months later, I was interrupted during a Board meeting by my PA. This very rarely happens and I was annoyed at first. But then I discovered why the intrusion was necessary. Mother Teresa was downstairs and demanding to see me. I apologized to the Board and asked for a ten-minute recess. In the lobby, Mother Teresa was surrounded by employees paying their respects but she marched over to me as soon as I appeared. She then instructed me—it was that firm, she didn't really ask—that all wasted food on Alitalia flights to India be given to the Missionaries of Charity. I happily agreed and said that as the Chairman of the Association of European Airlines (AEA) for 1991 I would ask all my colleagues to join me in this initiative.

She left pleased but unfortunately we were prevented from complying with her wishes as the Indian authorities couldn't allow it due to the local health regulations.

Fashion statement

Early on at Alitalia, I also got some free fashion lessons from one of the world's great designers, Giorgio Armani. He had won a competition to design our new uniforms and advise on the cabin interiors of new aircraft. I was not very happy with his first efforts, however. All I saw was grey. There was barely a hint of the red, white and green that I was expecting as head of the national carrier of Italy. I wanted customers to recognize our crew at an airport. But then I looked again, closely. Only one word immediately came to mind: elegance. Grey wasn't the fashion at the time but it soon took hold. Giorgio was absolutely right in his instinct that a top-class uniform was more important than flashing some company colours. Seeing the crew walking together through the airport wearing the new uniforms blended elegance and Alitalia in the customer's mind—a real boost to the brand. To underline the point, about 24 months later my CFO came to me with a sizeable bill for some new coats. I couldn't believe it. Why were we having to spend out again so soon? "The female crew really love the coats," I was told. "They're being worn when they go out socially." I was happy to sign the check knowing that. You can't beat that sort of publicity.

It was hard won though. My friend and very competent Director General, Ferruccio Pavolini, told me at the end of the process, "Giovanni, this job involving a famous designer, our cabin crew, and the CFO has been harder than opening a new route!"

We also had grey carpets on the new MD11 planes. It was a series of different tones, starting with a very light grey near the forward doors. The trouble was this got dirty very quickly. "No problem," I said. "Just alter the sequence of the tones so we start with a darker grey." When Giorgio found out he was not at all pleased. Unwittingly, I had changed a very carefully crafted design.

The new aircraft were a success despite my fashion *faux pas*. At the time, aircraft were available at favorable rates and Alitalia became a launch customer for the Airbus A320 and MD-11 in Europe. This allowed us to improve our route network and we began nonstop services from Rome to Buenos Aires, Miami and Los Angeles. In the meantime, we restructured the management. It was painful but we did it fast—like taking a band-aid off.

Positive thinking

As mentioned, we were already having trouble because IRI had refused to invest the requisite capital for the new planes. We then got hit by the 1990 Iraq invasion of Kuwait. We were heavily exposed in the Middle East and were among the few airlines without any government assistance to rely on. Legislation meant we couldn't reduce the workforce or the network. Every morning the management team met in my office at 10am and it's fair to say I've been at livelier funerals. We did manage to reduce costs to a degree but it was really just a drop in the ocean. The tipping point came when we flew two people from New York to Rome and one of them was the Director General of the Italian Treasury. He had no choice about when to fly or on which airline.

I worked out we had four months' worth of cash in the bank. If the war hadn't ended by then we would go bust. It was that stark. But if the war did end in time, we needed to hit the ground running. So that's where I focused my attention. Apart from keeping down costs, I couldn't do anything while the war was going on, so it was best to direct my energies positively and look at what we could do once it ended. Starting immediately, I told the team I would run the airline on a day-to-day basis with a small team. Everybody else was instructed to work on the "day after" plan.

Initially the strategy didn't get a warm welcome. "Giovanni is crazy, we should be working hard on day-to-day operations to limit the damage as much as possible" was the gist. The mood wasn't helped by the fact that the "day after" management were told to work outside headquarters. Still, after a couple of weeks, they submitted their proposals. These, of course, necessitated some investment on the airline's part. I'm sure they all expected me to say we couldn't afford it. We couldn't afford it—but I doubled the amounts they were asking for anyway. The ideas were good and deserved my full backing. We quickly identified teams for each Middle East country and it would be their job to get that market back up to speed in an instant. Significant market share gains were at stake as we also looked at potential new destinations. The mood brightened considerably and ideas began to flow.

Fortunately, the war ended soon after and Alitalia doubled its Middle East market share, with high yields replenishing our coffers in record time to boot. Our competitors had cut back massively and it took them time to scale-up their operations. Even Lufthansa was struggling near bankruptcy at the time and this was when Jürgen Weber was called in to save the ship.

Alitalia was regaining its strength rapidly. We took over Hungarian carrier Malev to operate as a low-cost alternative on new intercontinental routes. I was also becoming active in the Association of European Airlines, particularly in regard to deregulation debates. This would enable airlines to choose their European routes on a commercial basis rather than be dictated to by nonsense government rules. Basically, northern airlines, lead by Colin Marshall at British Airways, were keen for a quick process while Southern European airlines were more reserved. The stand-off was at its height when I was elected Chairman of the AEA. I worked with the European Commissioner, Karel van Miert, on a staged approach that soothed furrowed Southern European brows and mollified Northern European expectations by providing clear targets and a clear timeframe.

I had managed to build a consensus among airlines in a transparent manner, gaining the full support of the European Commission in the process. I told our members: "Today, airlines are politically strong and together we can influence our governments on the best solutions for the industry. If we wait, governments will decide for us and we cannot accept pre-cooked decisions." A couple of decades later and we have indeed been mismanaged by governments. Pre-cooked decisions have been as commonplace as pre-cooked meals in a supermarket.

With Alitalia performing well and my stint as head of the AEA showing progress, I started to do some keynote speeches at industry conferences, presenting a powerful image of the new-look Alitalia. Other airlines were keen to rub shoulders. KLM invited me to Amsterdam to evaluate areas of cooperation. In between presentations, two slides got stuck in the projector. The screen showed Alitalia's network superimposed over the KLM network. Jan de Soet, CEO of KLM, and I held our breath for a moment. There was very little overlap; the networks were complementary. With Power Points on personal computers I suppose such serendipity is a thing of the past. Anyway, we didn't make a song and dance of it but I began working with Jan and his successor, Peter Bouw, to see if we could join our operations. Soon enough, I informed the Alitalia Board of our intentions and the two airlines began a study in earnest, identifying the opportunities ahead.

After a few months of intensive work, I received a phone call from Carlo Bernini, my Minister of Transport and by far the most effective I worked with during my Alitalia days. He told me that the Minister of Transport for Sweden had called him suggesting that Alitalia should join SAS, Swissair and Austrian. The three carriers had been trying to build marketing mass through the European Quality Alliance. This gave rise to talks of a full merger, known as the Alcazar Project. But I explained to my Minister that the Alcazar Project would never get off the ground with so many different interests involved. Alitalia refused the Swedish Minister's offer but KLM accepted to join the talks, ending the discussion with Alitalia. Not long after Alcazar collapsed because, as anticipated, the airlines couldn't agree on a common strategy. Nor could they agree on a US partner, which they felt was necessary to get true economies of scale. Unfortunately, this led to the resignation of the SAS CEO, Jan Carlzon. He was a real visionary and had a very positive influence on the industry. Jan's emphasis on the passenger was exactly right but the market just wasn't ready for his progressive ideas. And believe me, thinking about the passenger was progressive at this point in time. Airlines had so much else on their plate to worry about.

There was great potential in airline cooperation, however, and, following KLM's withdrawal, I turned to Bernard Attali, CEO of Air France. Several meetings took place and we often spent weekends together working through a potential deal. The Saratoga Plan, as it was called, was hot enough to get plenty of unexpected media attention, which held back negotiations. In the end, Bernard left Air France before the deal could be done and I left Alitalia soon after that. I was touting a new business plan, which made a fresh confrontation with the unions inevitable. The Board understood and supported the strategy. It was the only way to ensure our competitiveness. But an Italian general election was looming and a union wrangle wasn't exactly the sexy, vote-winning strategy the politicians had in mind. My enthusiasm fizzled out with this political sidestep. I told IRI that my plan was the only way forward and so had no choice but to resign. The entire Alitalia Board left with me in support.

Call of the seas

I was still an IRI employee and the powers that be decided I was needed at Tirrenia di Navigazione, a large shipping company. Again, I had been awarded a job where change was paramount. Tirrenia mainly operated ferries between

Italy and islands in the Mediterranean. It served over 20 million passengers every year but its fleet of ships was very old. So I put forward a business plan to the Board that focused on revolutionary, faster ships.

We began by fitting some new jet aircraft GE engines to improve the speed of our ferries. The connection time to Sardinia from the Italian mainland was reduced from an overnight crossing to just three hours. It meant we needed only 30 crew rather than 100 and we could run five times a day. The move was well received—by passengers and unions alike. It was understood this was the only acceptable way forward and saved a company that had a history dating back to the 19th century. I asked a union leader why a massive restructuring, like the one at Tirrenia, could happen with little, if any, industrial action, while a similar situation at an airline would always result in disruption, whether in Europe, the United States or Japan.

He had a simple answer. "Pilots and flight crew stay in high-class hotels, and have a lot of free time in which to discuss salary and working conditions with colleagues from other parts of the world," he said. "They don't have a direct relationship with the company, just communicating by faxes to confirm a flight plan. It's a disconnected life. In a shipping company, the Captain and crew consider the ship their second family. They sometimes live aboard for months and they become very connected with the vessel and the company."

I've often mentioned this conversation to airline CEOs because a pilot's attitude is common throughout the world, from Japan to Latin America. It continues to be a key issue. The airline relationship with its pilots must be improved.

In the 1990s, the desire for privatization took hold. We weren't even immune from this irresistible force at IRI. Although Tirrenia was a long way down the privatization list, I knew I wasn't the type of person who could sit around waiting for an industrial empire to be dismantled. So I accepted an offer from GE and Group Serra to form SM Logistics, which was essentially a merger between two older, well-respected entities, Merzario and Serra. These two companies had operated in the shipping, trucking and freight forwarding sectors since the turn of the century and covered a vast geographic area. It had to be completed quickly to ensure the benefits were realized. This was done but it was a difficult task because the companies had decades of history as fierce rivals.

Call of the skies

I was living between Milan and Genoa while trying to achieve this convoluted merger. I was still keeping close ties with the airline industry and some old colleagues, particularly Jürgen Weber at Lufthansa. He had managed to turn around an airline on the verge of collapse. And Lufthansa has gone from strength to strength.

During a long weekend in the United States, Jürgen and the then Air France CEO, Jean-Cyril Spinetta, mentioned that they were teaming up with British Airways to take advantage of new opportunities in distribution via the Internet. They felt I could make a contribution to the project. I was intrigued and we talked about the idea endlessly, lost in the relaxing atmosphere of the Wyoming mountains that had graced many a Western film. Another challenge was looming, another big gamble.

Starting a fresh project in a completely new arena, which the Internet was at the time, held plenty of appeal. My previous roles had all been about big companies, big staff and big revenues. Every company I had worked for was rich in history and tradition. But this was a relatively modest affair operating in a novel environment. Still, Jean-Cyril's and Jürgen's involvement in a pioneering Internet company was a sure sign that this was a serious project. I knew Jean-Cyril well from my days at Alitalia. He had been CEO of Air Inter and our paths had crossed many times. Perhaps because Jean-Cyril's parents were Corsican we became good friends and I had learned to trust his judgment. Later, when he became CEO of Air France, he served as Chairman of the IATA Board and provided fantastic support for me. He also had the vision to be the first airline CEO to push through a major merger. The Air France–KLM deal wasn't easy but Jean-Cyril had the courage to make it happen. Jürgen took over Lufthansa in 1991. The airline wasn't in the best shape and had been too interested in gaining market share in emerging destinations, such as China. The balance sheet was suffering as a result. Jürgen turned the company around but his judgment is best summed up by the two people he immediately called on to help him. Wolfgang Mayrhuber and Christoph Franz went on to become CEOs of the airline and under their leadership Lufthansa has continued to impress.

Rod Eddington at British Airways was also convinced that a new distribution channel was necessary and during a lunch at BA's headquarters effectively sold the project to me.

I arrived in London in 2000 to take up the new position. OPODO had taken on a wonderful building in Covent Garden and I had the team of McKinsey consultants waiting for me with their business plan. It wasn't my normal method of working to say the least but their involvement was helping to loose airline fingers off of the purse strings.

The first bit of news wasn't the best though. McKinsey said they had two weeks with me and then after that it was up to me to deliver the most advanced European travel portal in only ten months together with some impressive start-up figures on market penetration and revenue. I knew the Internet was a fast-moving world but this was speed of light. And for that added bit of spice there were only two OPODO employees when I started: me and a security guy on the door. I got some comfort from the business plan though and the fact that the airlines had decided to put $300 million into the project. These were better times for the industry, remember.

There were other positives. London was a great venue for an Internet start-up as it had a great pool of talent. My first choice was a Human Resources Director, Peter Carroll. He had great knowledge of the Internet world and proved very effective. Other key positions were quickly filled. Nicolas de Santis became my Marketing Director and cleverly avoided expensive TV deals and concentrated instead on a massive campaign on the London Underground and buses. The strategy clearly worked because we had a record number of hits on the day we went live.

Despite these successes, I started to have some concerns when it came to recruiting the software experts. This was a long, long way from my traditional background. These people dressed very differently and had some outlandish attitudes. It was really difficult to make a proper assessment of their skills. Were OPODO's technical challenges too much for them—or too boring?

We were paying well and we had attracted the best people from all over the world. There was little doubt that all the candidates were extremely bright but I worried that their interest was purely technical. Once that challenge had been met I feared they would be off to find the next cutting-edge project. We were only going to be a small team so I was wary of high staff turnover in the future.

In the end, the hiring process turned out perfectly and we had an amazing team that created a real buzz in the office. We never had more than 150 people at OPODO and yet the nature of the company meant each personality was distinct and a world away from traditional business norms. Creativity was encouraged but staff had to be constructive too. A tight-knit team ethic was essential. T-shirts, jeans and sandals were *de riguer*. I was the one out of place in a suit. Looking after some 30,000 employees in my earlier role at Alitalia was a breeze in comparison. Yet, there was never any cause to complain. We built a great team and they outperformed every target that was set.

If a problem got their attention they would work day and night to solve it. Jill Brady, who moved on to Virgin Atlantic, was General Counsel at OPODO at the time and spent many long nights reviewing the software contracts with Sapient, each of which was the size of an encyclopedia.

The technical platform on the original business plan was good but it was too expensive. The numbers didn't stack up. I spoke about it to the shareholders. "If I want to run an inexpensive taxi service in London and be competitive, I can't go out and buy a fleet of Rolls Royces," I stormed. This seemed to catch their attention but the matter was taken out of my hands somewhat by 9/11. Cost reduction became inevitable. Despite that disruption we launched the most innovative, powerful travel website in Europe on time. And we surpassed every target. In Germany, only the Deutsche Bahn website had more hits.

OPODO has now been sold and companies like Google are entering the airline distribution sector. As I mentioned before, airlines often have great ideas but never the finances to see them through to completion. How an airline ticket gets sold is still a great challenge.

Time to start work

OPODO and all my previous jobs had given me some great insights. So when the IATA position was offered I knew I had something to offer. I had international experience, airline experience and inside knowledge of a powerful new business tool. I also brought with me personal links with many of the movers and shakers of this world.

It was this last attribute that finally brought home the meaning of Leo Mullin's call for relevance. IATA shouldn't be speaking with Civil Aviation Authorities. We needed to be speaking with Prime Ministers, Presidents and the Secretary General of the United Nations.

If IATA was to build the necessary consensus to achieve change at breakneck speed then leadership and interaction at the highest level would have to be the magic wand.

I accepted the job as IATA Director General and CEO in February 2002 and received unanimous approval from the IATA Board a month later.

CHAPTER TWO
Internal Combustion

Making internal changes at IATA

Blowing away cobwebs

I arrived at IATA's Executive Office in Geneva as IATA Director General and CEO designate on 15 May 2002. Preparations for the June AGM in Shanghai, where my position would be formally approved, were in full swing. I paid great attention to what was going on, the role of the various committees and the general atmosphere.

Pierre Jeanniot briefed me, detailing his frustration with the more complex aspects of IATA's responsibilities. I patiently took note and refrained from making comment. I also began a series of interviews with the top 50 managers, looking in vain for a rationale behind the current system. If there was any logic at all, it appeared to be "stop change at all costs!"

Although I expected that attitude in Geneva, I was still shocked by the Shanghai AGM itself. I knew the association had been gathering dust but things were far worse than I anticipated. IATA was enveloped in a thick smog of inaction. There was nothing new at the AGM—the single most important event in IATA's calendar. Its structure hadn't seen the light of day for a long time. It was long, bureaucratic and totally prescribed with no room for debate of the major issues of the day.

Remember, airlines were collapsing under the effects of 9/11. Many had already gone bust, many were about to go bust, and much of the remainder was desperate for government aid. The Shanghai meeting barely acknowledged this incredible situation. In my acceptance speech, I made it clear that quiet diplomacy would not get air transport out of this mess. "The challenges must be communicated strongly, clearly and effectively in order to influence the wider political and economic community," I said. "We in IATA must have the courage to use all our strengths, our passion and our global reputation to make things happen. And happen quickly. We must use our skills, authority and breadth of access to present viable and sustainable options to governments and international organizations in the most compelling way."

The day after the Shanghai AGM, I flew to Singapore for my first official meeting as Director General of IATA. There was a different atmosphere in the office there. Singapore is an entrepreneurial city; you can breathe the innovation just walking down the street. And aviation in Asia-Pacific was about to start moving at a different pace. I think the Singapore office understood that and was excited by the prospect.

Unfortunately, IATA's decision-making process wasn't in Singapore. It was in Geneva and Montreal. The *raison d'être* of the main offices was clearly to maintain the status quo: "Why change? We are IATA, an association. We are not an airline, we are not running a business and we were not hit by the crisis."

So I knew where to start.

Ending the committee excuse

Returning to Geneva, I resumed my one-to-one interviews with all the IATA managers. My day started at 8am and ended at 10pm. There was no deputy to assist me—it would have to be all my own work. I had to act fast but I also wanted to give everyone a chance to present me with their suggestions. I explained to them that IATA needed speed, passion and commitment. Give me that and they could be part of the new team.

Too often, though, I heard the same arguments. A not-for-profit organization must not make money, an association must follow and not lead. These arguments, I was told, had their roots in discussions with the airline members and IATA's mind-boggling array of committees.

The committee concept wasn't wrong as such. Once, these committees, which covered a variety of aviation topics, had provided an effective link between IATA and the airlines, especially for safety and operational discussions. But time moves on. Rather than an open forum the committees had become closed shops. Although it was a tough challenge, moving against this committee structure was unavoidable if there was to be any sort of progress at IATA.

At the following Board meeting I told the members we needed to review the situation immediately. Kevin Dobby, the brilliant IATA Corporate Secretary, was asked to provide the full, sorry picture on my behalf. An incredible patchwork of more than 150 committees, special conferences and working groups came to light, most of them with no real input into the industry. All they did was give their members a chance to chat with old colleagues in various wonderful locations around the world. I have no idea what the Time Limit Working Group discussed or the Global Consultative Committee or the Flight Interruption Manifest Work Group. There were around 25 committees and working groups in cargo alone.

The committees were supposed to discuss policy issues but they also had to approve targets for related divisions and organize a schedule of country/airline visits. They were micro-managing the whole industry.

I asked Board members Jürgen Weber of Lufthansa and CK Cheong of Singapore Airlines, two strong agents of change, to assist me. I proposed to cut the number of committees as well as limit the number of participants to 12 per committee, with the exception of the Operations Committee with 20 members. Most of the airlines didn't agree with the cuts, no doubt influenced by those who no longer had free trips overseas. And of course the structure had been in place for decades. The mindset was well established and not easy to change. I sensed the objections were a momentary sulk, however. Nobody seriously doubted the logic of the move.

BA's Rod Eddington helped gain Board support for the next step even though he had to fight his own internal battle in BA. Plenty of its staff didn't want IATA to change its way. The airlines were invited to put forward candidates for the committees and I would pick the most suitable combination. I wanted to ensure the committees we allowed to survive would actually have some purpose and challenge IATA to move forward. It may sound arrogant but these were early days and I had to show we were going to be a different association. No longer would IATA be hostage to the committees.

Strangely, some airlines have recently asked for a return to the past using transparency as a code word for the micro-management of an industry through endless committees. I hope IATA is strong enough in the future to support only those changes that help the association deliver positive results. Industry politics and a place on the IATA Board should not be a key priority for anybody.

A strange animal

Dealing with the committees was a start but it was just that: a start. Much more was needed. But how do you articulate a vision and strategy for an association? IATA was, and still is, a unique animal.

Normally the role of an association in a business environment is linked to its influence on decision-makers. Ideally, it should facilitate the development of the industry that it represents. The associations of the car industry, the banking sector and so on are essentially lobby groups that interface with governments, lawmakers and consumer associations. The industry tells the association what it needs and then its association gets to work.

IATA is different. It has a far more comprehensive role and is truly entwined with the aviation industry, heavily involved in the distribution and financial settlement of the product. It handles more than $300 billion every year on behalf of the airlines and is among the largest private clients in the banking sector. This peculiarity stems from IATA's history. The first IATA was established in 1919 and was essentially about improving safety levels. Aviation had few constraints at that time. There were no bilateral agreements, no ownership rules. Europeans could own US carriers, for example—something just not possible today.

In 1944, the Chicago Convention prescribed new rules, heavily influenced by events in the Second World War. At the same time, the International Civil Aviation Organization (ICAO) became a specialized United Nations agency. A revamped version of IATA was inaugurated in Havana, Cuba a year later to facilitate the new set-up.

Safety was, is and always will be the most important priority. When IATA began in 1945, the airlines carried 9 million passengers and there were 247 fatalities. In 2011, 2.3 billion passengers took to the skies and there were 486 fatalities. The Western-built jet hull loss rate for 2012 was at a record low of 0.20 per million flights (or one hull loss for every 5 million flights). Flying is the safest way to travel and we've made it even safer.

Originally, though, this laudable emphasis on safety had some bizarre side effects. Because governments didn't want competition to unduly affect cooperative efforts to make the skies safer, IATA was charged with establishing a whole series of protocols, standards and tariffs to govern the industry. Special inspectors flew anonymously to check the prices, meals and services provided were in accordance with IATA regulations. When on board they had to show their IATA credentials and there was panic among the crews as everything from the pitch of the seat to the size of the cushions and food portions was checked. It led to some farcical confrontations, the most famous—or should that be infamous—of which was the Great Sandwich War of 1958, when TWA and Pan Am took exception to the better fillings offered by a few European carriers. The comedy continued with a two-day IATA conference in London that deemed that member airlines' economy class sandwiches must be cold and free of garnishes or fancy ingredients. Some might say airline food is still far from fancy but at least they are now free to make their own decisions about their meals. IATA wasn't too upset by these schoolboy rows. It got to fine the airlines every time they sidestepped the rules and that's how the association made its money.

IATA's first DG was Sir Hildred William, the former British representative at the Chicago Convention, but it was under the leadership of the second DG, Knut Hammarsjöld, that IATA started to expand its activities. The most important development was probably the IATA Clearing House, which revolutionized distribution. Any passenger in the world, through the 70,000 or so IATA-accredited agents, could buy an IATA airline ticket in their local currency and have it accepted by IATA members. And if the airline went bankrupt, IATA would reimburse the passenger.

The third DG, Günther Eser, launched training and consulting activities and greatly expanded membership while my immediate predecessor, Pierre Jeanniot, was able to take charge of the industry settlement system that was initially handled by local carriers in IATA's name.

Step by step, the association had moved serenely forward, broadening its role, setting technical standards and publishing enormous amounts of information on all things aviation.

Why become relevant?

For all their efforts though, previous IATA DGs had found their hands tied by the nature of the association. IATA was intrinsic to the industry itself and any change was hard won. My situation was different in that the status quo could no longer be maintained. Something, somewhere was going to snap under the pressure of a wave of global crises and new market dynamics.

If I was to fulfill Leo Mullin's original brief to be relevant to a modern industry, the old dog that was IATA had to be taught new tricks.

Assisting the airlines in improving their business brought to mind three crucial goals for IATA:

- *Increase safety levels and help the industry aim for zero fatalities.*
- *Help airlines reduce their costs by setting up new processes and standards and negotiating better deals with airports and air navigation service providers.*
- *Make governments understand that healthy competition would be the most effective means of governing the industry.*

It wasn't easy, partly due to the stubbornness of those defending the status quo and partly because there were some complex problems. The depth of sandwich fillings was the least of my problems. I had to turn IATA into an association capable of supporting my change agenda.

The right tools for the job

IATA had to make a difference. But if you want to change an industry, the minimum needed is the right set of tools. The IATA I inherited reflected the bureaucracy of the last 50 years and the state of the industry at large. It was stuffy, outdated, inefficient and highly insular. IATA typified airline thinking that this was an industry comprehensible only to insiders. But the world had changed and aviation had to change with it if it was to continue facilitating stronger cultural and social ties and encourage economic growth.

IATA employees were generally ex-airline staff, many of whom were simply marking time before retirement in the risk-free arena of a trade association. This was especially true of senior management. Having missed out on the top rung of the ladder at a major airline they had shuffled sideways for a cozy life. Worse, they had brought major airline thinking with them. Shrinking this narrow thinking even further was the fact that Board members overwhelmingly represented the biggest airlines.

The IATA cultural make-up was equally limited. When I arrived well over 60% of staff were British, American or Canadian. This was hardly the staff of a global association—and I knew it would not fly in a world spinning towards globalization.

Cultural diversity and cultural knowledge are essential to effective business on a global scale. It is easier said than done, of course. Different attitudes and practices have to be blended into a coherent whole and initially there is bound to be resistance. And resistance was exactly what I encountered when I arrived at IATA.

IATA is a small organization in terms of staff numbers—just 1,500 to 2,000. But it operates approximately 80 offices worldwide. Its job is to represent airlines in every corner of the globe, small carriers as well as big. It is the only non-political organization in the world—including the United Nations—that has members in the People's Republic of China and Taiwan.

To fulfill its mission, IATA has to defend its members under any circumstances, without fear or favour. Afrique Airways, Syrian Air and Iran Air all suffered when sanctions were imposed on their home states by the international community. We had to insist on access to spare aircraft parts to ensure safety, which under the ICAO Convention cannot have boundaries or political limitations. I personally explained this crucial clause and the industry's safety priority to the US State Department and the European Commission on several occasions. We were successful in getting spare parts to Afrique Airways in Libya and to Syrian Air but failed to help Iran Air in 2010 after a congressional vote ensured the sanctions remained in place. We had to suspend the airline from the industry systems.

When I joined IATA, however, I felt the association's ability to represent the industry was severely limited. Incredibly, IATA had done its best to pretend that the winds of change would blow themselves out. Nearly all IATA staff, it seemed, still did not appreciate that the time had come to change their skills, their processes, in fact their entire cultural approach. For them, it was simply a matter of biding time until "business as usual" could be resumed.

I realized I had to hit where it really hurt.

A bomb in the church

If IATA and the airlines it represented were not completely divorced then certainly it was a marriage on the rocks. I wanted a sense of urgency, a wake-up call that was brutally effective. Speed wasn't just a Giovanni trademark. It was absolutely essential to survival. If we hadn't started to make a difference within the first year then the association, and perhaps even the industry, would be on their last legs, awaiting the knockout blow.

In terms of internal reorganization, that meant targeting both the staff and the structure. I needed to expose the senior management to a new corporate culture and make them understand that the world had changed. There is only one way to deal with people who think their job is not at risk: put their job at risk. I was going to change IATA, and change it quickly. If staff couldn't accept that then there would be no place for them in the association.

I made my first management presentation in July 2002, one month after I took office. It contained the following key points:

- *Speed, passion and commitment would be essential.*
- *Teamwork, change and communication would lead to a new management style.*
- *Real targets would make IATA a results-focused association.*
- *Management would face a tough and fast assessment.*
- *Anybody left behind would be lost to the association.*

It was a terrible shock to the system of some, I'm sure. At the time, I think I only had three true believers: Tom Windmuller, a brilliant young manager who would rise to become Corporate Secretary; my first PA, Conchita Greiner; and Dominique Durand, who went on to work for me throughout my time at IATA and who provided tireless, intelligent support.

I sensed that most were thinking this was just another episode that could be ridden out. I had clear ideas about how to change that mindset but it never hurts to get a second opinion. I turned again to Jack Welch. GE is a great organization and its leadership programs have always been at the vanguard of any change process. The management style implemented by Jack is by far the most effective, anywhere. Management and corporate culture programs were so important to Jack that he personally attended training on a frequent basis. Every month he would spend at least a day or two at GE's legendary business school in Crotonville, New York. Sessions there are tough; it's not about making, or politely listening to, a presentation. Managers are put into a boxing ring and taught how to fight in a discussion. Their future depends on how they perform.

The ringmaster at Crotonville is Noel Tichy, Dean of the GE Business School, and the most prominent professor at the Ann Arbor University Business School in Michigan. I wanted Noel to put IATA management on the ropes but I wasn't sure a crusty association held any interest for him. And I also needed to justify the cost to a board that wasn't authorizing more than $1,000 a year on management programs.

I called Jack. I explained the situation was more or less what I had anticipated when we had met in New York. Jack noted that the strength of the GE management program was a major factor in the company's powerful performance across all their activities. Whether this would translate to an association was another matter, he added.

I insisted. I had to take the risk. I had to try to succeed where the world-shaping events of the early 21st century had failed.

Jack was a great help to me. He met with Noel Tichy and managed to persuade him to begin a very different type of adventure with IATA.

I explained my ideas to Xavier de Irala, who had taken over from Leo Mullin as IATA's Chairman and was, coincidentally, a former GE manager. He knew Noel and had survived the tough challenges at Crotonville. After I told him that Noel was coming, he reflected silently for a couple of minutes and then said: "I hope it works." I smiled back: "It will be like putting a bomb in a church."

There was a real chance that the plan could derail and simply collapse the association entirely. But if IATA didn't change that was its eventual fate anyway, so this adrenalin injection was worth a shot.

Leaders developing leaders

Through the Executive Management Group (EMG), I implemented the Senior Team Alignment Process (STAP). We would work around the key themes of our people, our members and our organization. I also added a magical new word to the IATA lexicon. From now on we wouldn't just represent and serve. We would "represent, lead and serve". The Board accepted this change quietly but underestimated what the concept of leadership would mean. And they certainly underestimated how I would use it.

At our second STAP workshop, the EMG identified 47 participants for what we termed the IATA Change Leadership (ICL) program. This program would be facilitated by Noel's Brimstone team. It was not just current senior staff taking part. We took pains to include the leaders of tomorrow as well. The idea was simple: get a small group of strong personnel that fully embraced the changes to influence a large middle group of employees who were still unsure about the transformation before finally battling the small group at the other extreme who were actively opposed.

I made it my mission to attend all the ICL workshops but this was a concept that thrived on its own merits. We were offering a chance for staff to increase their skillset, their earning power and their career potential. It was also an "all-in" program, where staff of all levels mixed and worked together. It was a great experience for everybody though initially it may have been a touch uncomfortable for the senior Chinese Director challenged by an outspoken young Canadian Assistant Manager. They were playing a management game, where you give directions to somebody to guide them along a course. The Chinese Director was blindfolded but was still trying to direct operations much to the Canadian's dismay. She was making it quite clear where the power now lay: with her! He insisted he was told her name and that he would report the case. To him, this was an insult and we had to talk him down from a very high horse.

The program was shocking for some. But while there were several cases of emotional tension, no participant left before the end of the program. The Chinese office still has its own identity but is fully aligned with the IATA culture and the Chinese Director, Baojian Zhang, has done a great job. He is now a Regional Vice President.

ICL developed many new ideas for IATA. Teams presented viable, real world projects and the Executive Management decided which ones would be retained. The projects automatically became a priority for the responsible departments. Some of the most important work we have done for the industry—Simplifying the Business and the IATA Operational Safety Audit, for example—were fleshed out in ICL sessions.

Performance assessment

Our people-first strategy was a real about-turn for IATA. The previous system of performance analysis (PA) was quite literally pointless because staff scores were completely ignored. They had no bearing on pay, bonuses or potential terminations. Divisions even had different versions of the PA form and less than half of the employees had fully completed forms in their personnel files.

To create a successful IATA, the focus needed to shift from processes to results. Managers needed to be decisive and clearly distinguish between strong and weak performers in their teams.

We adapted the classic GE approach. Those marked A were the star performers, B staff could do better but deserved our perseverance, while members of the C group probably had no further part to play in IATA's future. It was the leadership quality that we required of every employee that proved to be the real game-changer. With so many new commercial services in the pipeline as well as our new philosophy, staff had to operate from the front. They had to lead the way in a brave new world.

A different organization

The training sessions with Noel Tichy and his Brimstone team helped align senior managers with the many challenges we faced. It allowed us to revise the IATA mission, vision and values. But there was always more to be done. We had to make sure the structure was efficient enough to bring a different business approach in the quickest possible time. IATA was now going to lead the industry and I had to translate that concept into reality.

I flattened the structure considerably, from an average near nine layers per division down to less than six, and I moved Human Resources to a direct report to me. The move was crucial because I flattened a lot of staff too. This was part of the structural shift. I needed to realign some divisions and ensure staff had enough experience and gravitas to give IATA the impetus for change at industry level.

Reforming HR into a key agent of change required a head of department with skills in change management and international experience. I discussed this with the existing HR Director and explained the role both he and his department would need to play in implementing IATA's new management style. He listened carefully and then suggested I should rethink the strategy. He was convinced this wouldn't work in an association and wouldn't be understood by our member airlines. I appreciated his honesty but it was obvious that I had met my first hurdle. I fired him with immediate effect. "From tomorrow, you are out," I said. "The legal department will handle the follow-up." I brought in Guido Gianasso, who had experience in international organizations, most recently with Credit Suisse. He has made a significant contribution to the new-look IATA.

A strong signal, such as the dismissal of a "blocker", can be worth a thousand meetings. I always try to work with the existing staff but if change doesn't come quickly enough, I'm prepared to move up a gear.

The new structure also had to overcome boundaries. There were two types of recalcitrant staff when I joined IATA that I called silo experts and club meds. Silo experts were more common. They would sit in their office, confident they couldn't be touched because of their specialized knowledge. This singular intelligence meant communicating with colleagues was pointless or beneath them. Our financial services division was particularly resplendent with silo experts. It was their indifference to the team ethic that held back our global network and the support needed in regional offices.

I had repeatedly stressed that change was urgent but one silo expert held firm. One day I called in Tom Murphy, the Senior Vice President of the division. "Your Director of IATA Settlement Systems (ISS) will be fired today," I said. Tom was shocked. This director was considered a guru in his field and it was feared that losing him would create some kind of financial black hole. I didn't alter my opinion and once he was gone, the restructuring of the ISS gathered the necessary pace.

Meanwhile, the club meds were having a wonderful life. These staff were travelling around the regions to remind people that IATA still existed but had no targets or strategy. So when Bob Hutt, the Chief Financial Officer, came to me with an urgent issue about the club meds, I grabbed the opportunity to rock their boat. Bob was concerned that they weren't turning in their travel expenses on time. I was surprised this was deemed an urgent issue but offered a simple solution: immediately suspend the company credit card of anyone not following the proscribed reporting rules. It wasn't my prime concern if people had to hitchhike home. The RVP of Africa had to pay for his own flight and then a train home, which can't have been easy. Bob was amazed at such drastic action and some club meds were put out by having to find their own fare home, but the problem was remedied rather quickly.

Early on, I also got a new Head of Marketing and Commercial Services (MACS), employing Mark Hubble as a Senior Vice President. The previous occupant worked out of Montreal but had, for reasons beyond me, built up a large department in London, one of the most expensive cities in the world. The new appointment made structural changes much easier and MACS now touches on every division. Mark opened up new commercial opportunities for IATA and this has made a tremendous difference to our financial model. A matrix structure has enabled IATA to utilize the expertise embedded in its divisions and targets have made the department truly effective. From 2004–11 we doubled our commercial revenues.

In my first year in charge, 246 staff left IATA and 127 joined. I vetted all of the new staff to make sure they were agents of change. They were coming in from top organizations such as Barclays Bank, Credit Suisse, GE and IBM, so we were moving in the right direction. Coupled with the Brimstone training, it meant that by end 2003 my new management team was more or less complete. Only once did I not have the time to interview personally a candidate. I asked my management team which of the three candidates they preferred. They all looked blank. Kevin Dobby spoke up: "I've never been asked that before," he said, surprised. "We usually just hire the cheapest!"

IATA was by no means alone in business in this policy. But it had to change. For IATA, its staff were its only asset. It was essential to pick the best. This wasn't just a shock internally. Any headhunters we worked with also told me that IATA didn't have a lot of sex appeal and "the best" would be hard to persuade. But gradually the tide turned. Word was spreading that a revolution in IATA had begun.

From 2003–07, some 20% of the staff changed on an annual basis—and this in an organization that had a long history of no firings and minimal staff turnover. Overall, during the same period, over 1,000 people joined us and nearly 1,200 left. Some were sacked, some resigned because this wasn't the place for them. And quite a few were poached. We gave our people great training at places like Harvard and MIT and great experience in the global marketplace. This made them a desirable commodity. I don't mind staff being poached. In fact, I'm quite proud when it happens because it shows I'm on the right track.

But the numbers don't lie. Considering our total workforce of around 1,500, they show the bomb in the church had well and truly exploded.

Regional variations

It wasn't just about change at Geneva and Montreal. From the start I was aware that the global aspect of our operation wasn't strong enough. On my visits to the country offices—which, incidentally, were often the first by any IATA Director General—I had noticed that their role was limited to the handling of the settlement system. The heads of the offices were acting as accountants and staff were solely involved in settlement processes. We were barely scraping the surface in terms of their potential.

I started with the seven regional offices, ensuring they were true hubs for the country offices. As for the country offices themselves, their key priority became keeping in touch with member airlines, the regional offices and the main IATA offices in Montreal and Geneva. This would ensure a continuous two-way flow of information, anticipating and responding to needs as required. It led to the country offices having far more responsibility, as well as accountability, and they were soon in touch with the national governments and aviation authorities gathering vital information.

Within a year many of the country managers had been changed to reflect the offices' new-found importance. I seized the opportunity to raise the bar in terms of the qualifications for the role. No longer accountants, they would need the interpersonal skills to liaise with industry stakeholders across the board. I was even tougher on the heads of the regional offices. They had to be former airline CEOs. I wanted to make sure IATA had the necessary gravitas and that any regional discussions would be conducted at the proper level. Patricio Sepulveda, the Regional Vice President (RVP) for Latin America, was the only one with the necessary leadership and background, having been a CEO of LAN and an IATA Board member. He has always been a strong influence in the region. But increasing the quality of the RVPs was the right thing to do. Our worldwide network took a quantum leap in performance and we finally formed close links with the industry.

The next step was the offices themselves. They were often located in the cheapest parts of town, far from the action and far from safe. Not the right image for an organization looking to negotiate with world leaders. Giving IATA the image I wanted was an expensive investment but I had to underline the agenda for change in every aspect of our operations. We needed offices that wouldn't be an embarrassment to us when our aviation partners came calling. We needed offices that showed we meant business.

In Riyadh, Saudi Arabia, the office moved away from a not particularly good—but wonderfully pungent—food market. In Kiev, Ukraine, we lost an unlit room in the backyard of an old building. We hired an architect to ensure all our new offices had the same feel and made sure every visitor was aware that IATA had changed. All around the world, IATA staff are now happy to arrange meetings at the association's offices. The days of suggesting a coffee at a nearby hotel any time a member wanted to meet are finally over.

The value of leadership

Leadership makes all the difference to an organization. The goal is always sustainable growth and consistent profits. To achieve this I believe a good leader needs to motivate his team to achieve tough targets in the short term and to work toward a strategy and vision for the company in the long term.

Every organization is different, of course. At IATA, I had to take a prehistoric animal and adapt it to the modern world. But as I joined IATA at what was probably the lowest point in aviation history, I had a mandate for change. I applied some crucial leadership tips to three key areas: the internal structure and personnel; monopoly providers in the value chain; and governments.

Internally, as outlined earlier, I set tough targets and implemented a transparent performance assessment scheme. Just as importantly, I also embarked on a strategy of strong commercial growth. Although IATA is not-for-profit, I knew that my ability to transform the industry hinged on being able to take independent decisions. You can't control your business if you're always asking for money to implement a project.

In dealing with monopoly providers, it would sometimes seem that the target—most often driving down prices—was impossible to achieve. After all, how can you convince a third party to be cheaper when there are no alternatives? This is where a good leader has to step up and build the teamwork and commitment that keeps the organization driving forward. It makes the impossible, possible. The language you use can be very influential. I always tried to use the word "aspiration" rather than target when setting out my ideas. That gave me the time to build momentum before transforming that aspiration into a target. As I will explain later, this is exactly what I did when I presented the idea of making the industry carbon-neutral. I first won consensus that being carbon-neutral was a great aspiration. And then, with the aspiration established, I moved on to working out a path for that dream to become a reality, with targets along the way.

When it came to governments, I knew I had to move up the ladder and deal with the real decision-makers—Prime Ministers and Presidents rather than Ministers of Transport. It is becoming quite common for larger companies to have contact with governments, particularly those with worldwide networks. Big business is an important part of the global village. As with companies in other sectors, the destiny of an airline can depend on a political decision.

You need to be able to influence those decisions. My strategy was to talk first of related subjects where you know there is common ground. This establishes an understanding and makes an agreement at the end of the meeting more likely. And never close the door even if the meeting doesn't end favorably. There is always the possibility of a second chance.

Only if all else fails do you prepare for battle. And even then a leader must first make sure the equation makes sense. The reward must make the risk worthwhile. Of course, being a leader is about taking risks. You won't hit targets by standing still. The only time to be absolutely certain of the result is if it is your first battle in a new job. Then the leader must win, otherwise credibility becomes a real issue.

Ultimately, every leader develops a unique style. At IATA I soon became known for my "crazy ideas" and for "shouting politely". But my ideas were never crazy—they were calculated risks. And for some, my politeness was not always evident.

CHAPTER THREE
Making Waves

The first external warning shots,
views on airports

The Narita case

Shaking up IATA with a new management team was the main focus early on in my IATA career. But I knew I also had to make waves industry-wide if the association was to have an impact on airline fortunes.

As mentioned, I'm a great believer in personalizing business relationships wherever possible. If you work on an international basis, that means embracing different cultures is a must. But this "classic approach" doesn't always work. Rules are there to be broken. Breaking the ice in some business relationships sometimes requires turning up the heat.

If anything, though, even greater cultural sensitivity is required when you start breathing fire. It helps you to know where to hit and how hard. And it also helps you to know when to hit. The Narita International Airport case underlines this "last resort approach".

Narita was the main provider of international flights in Tokyo, Japan, and that gave it the latitude to act as it wished in terms of the fees charged to airlines. It basically had a monopoly and had become the world's most expensive airport. Landing charges failed to account for the fact that airline prices had dropped 40% since 1984. The Japanese Government supported the airport's stance and had no interest in pursuing any efficiency drives. Slots were constrained and management flexibility was non-existent. Airlines were losing money left, right and centre and they could no longer afford this arrogant posturing.

To make matters worse, privatization was on the cards. When things get privatized, a necessary first step is making the balance sheet look as wonderful as possible for potential new investors. The Minister of Land, Infrastructure, Transport and Tourism, Chikage Ogi, was a powerful lady. She was a former theater performer, part of the all-female troupe, Takarazuka Review, and was acting up to get the support of the banking system for the privatization process.

The time was right to hit Narita and for me to move up a gear at IATA. It was late 2002. I had been at the association a few months and I needed to move quickly to gain credibility. Speed was of the essence. I had plenty of ideas from my OPODO experience in the formative stage but member airlines and IATA staff needed to see we would be an important part of the value chain and an agent of change. As Leo Mullin had stipulated, they needed to see we were relevant. Internal changes were already apparent but I needed to take my message out to the industry.

I asked my user charges team what was the most difficult case they faced. Narita was the answer and so the airport became my symbolic target. Many members of the aviation value chain makes money apart from the airlines. Some airports return huge profit margins and airframe and engine manufacturers can make good money too. Airlines dream of scraping a double-digit return.

I figured that attacking one of the most entrenched monopolies in the world in one of the most conservative countries would be the biggest gamble I could take. Narita epitomized the bad behaviour seen in so many aviation suppliers. I had no time for Plan Bs, for in-depth analysis, for possible avenues of compromise. If IATA was going to take a leap forward, we had to take on the toughest challenges and win.

Blending Japan and Italy

To be honest, it was a leap with a parachute. I knew Japan and Japanese culture well so I had a good idea how much I was stirring things up. I had conducted three major deals there during my time at IRI. Not all were successful. The notable failure was a joint venture between the car manufacturers Alfa Romeo and Nissan. Alfa Romeo was a jewel in IRI's crown and had started production of a new car at its Naples plant. But

Alfa Romeo couldn't quite reach the same level of efficiency it had with other models and at other plants. IRI management decided to ask Nissan for assistance. Unfortunately, the idea fell flat. I don't think the Japanese ever adjusted to the Neapolitan way of life and they were seen as an outside, even interfering, force. In the end, the problems escalated and Alfa Romeo was sold off to Fiat.

A steel production deal was very different. Finsider, one of the largest steel companies in the world, had built a major plant in Taranto, in the south of Italy, which was based on a similar technology used by Nippon Steel in a plant just outside Tokyo. Again there was a problem with efficiency and again we got the Japanese over. We rebuilt a hotel near the plant in a Japanese style and the management group that came over was treated as part of the team rather than outside consultants. It was a resounding success and we achieved the efficiency levels we craved.

The third example falls somewhere between these two extremes. Hitachi and Ansaldo Medical were able to combine on digital medical scanning equipment without any undue effort. Scientists can converse fluently in numbers and formulas—it's a universal culture.

I needed all of this experience to attack Narita. As NASA would say, failure was not an option. I had to win.

I asked my Airport User Charges team at IATA for some assistance. "Some" was actually a little less than I got. Two months later I reorganized the team, getting rid of most of them, complaining that I wanted lions but had inherited a flock of chickens. They told me that the usual IATA methodology was to ask airlines to assess the level of airport efficiency. This suggested what figures to use for the discussion, and where a compromise might be reached. But the negotiation, they suggested, was usually worthless. Reductions and/or efficiency gains were seldom acquired. The third stage saw the DG get involved. He had to—and this still amazes me—*write a letter of complaint*. It could be strongly worded (small mercy) but inevitably generated a reply that simply expanded on the original airport feedback. A polite "go away and leave us alone—but don't forget to send a cheque!"

This, they told me, was the result of most negotiations. It wasn't a result. A result is a reduction in fees or an efficiency gain of some kind—or, even better, both. With the existing process such a waste of time, I had to take the lead. The user charges team suggested that I shouldn't expose myself to the risk of failure but I had a very different viewpoint. Leadership is about taking risks, about leading your soldiers into battle. And I knew that if I was successful it would give me the impetus to drive further change.

I had the perfect battleground. IATA had been invited to the Airports Council International (ACI—the airport equivalent of IATA) World Congress in Tokyo and I planned to seize the opportunity. The event was being held at the Tokyo Bay Sheraton, a Disneyland hotel, so it seemed only right to put on a show that exposed what I considered to be the unreal, "cartoon" world that Narita inhabited.

The basic procedure for Japanese meetings is well known. It is polite, formal and heavily structured. It is not usually a good thing to deviate from these well-established rules. Well, I was going to deviate. I was going to stand up on stage and publicly embarrass Narita with a wealth of facts and figures that exposed their overblown prices, their inefficiency and their failure to adhere to ICAO principles. I would tell them that IATA had no time for privatizations that allowed monopolistic behavior to continue, that Narita was the most expensive airport in the world, and that the government should wake up before it slides further into the doldrums.

The last line of the speech noted that IATA would continue to be an active player and a noisy player. If nobody else would wake up the Japanese government, I'd be happy to do it.

Shouting politely

About two weeks before the ACI event I was in Tokyo to receive an award from Prince Takamado on behalf of IATA for 50 years work with Japanese aviation. While there I discussed the situation with our member airline CEOs in the area. I told them that unless the Narita situation changed quickly and dramatically I would create chaos at the ACI event. I said they could decide not to participate at the ACI event if they felt it would be too awkward. I didn't blame Isao Kaneko, CEO of Japan Airlines and Chairman of the IATA Board, for the year when he suddenly remembered an appointment in China the same day as the ACI event.

But the only person who saw how far my speech would go, apart from my Corporate Communications Director, Tony Concil, was Andrew Drysdale, the IATA Regional Vice President for Asia-Pacific and formerly a successful CEO with Air Pacific. He strongly supported my approach and was given strict instructions not to leak a word of it. I had a meeting with the ACI Board prior to the conference opening and made some "soft" remarks to test the water. Even these were not well-received but that just fortified my decision to go for broke at the conference proper.

I held on to my true speech until the morning of the conference. It got distributed to the interpreters at 7am in the morning. By 7:30am, I had received a call from the Director General of ACI, Robert Aaronson, suggesting I modify the language. I refused and said that ACI would have to cancel my slot because I wasn't changing a word. But I warned Bob. If ACI did withdraw my invitation I would organize a press conference and tell the world's media what I thought anyway.

I got to speak. It was a packed room, over 1,000 delegates and media. I was following a keynote opening by the former Japanese Prime

Minister, Ryutaro Hashimoto. About five minutes in, I worked up to the crux of the matter. I accused the government of failing to prevent abuse of a dominant market position and said they had given the airport authorities "a license to print money". I said they should all wake up to the new economic reality and that monopolistic behaviour in the modern age was intolerable. As for the idea of privatizing this mess with the help of Japanese banks, that would meet with the strongest possible objections from the aviation community until we got the transparency and efficiency we craved. "Unless the Japanese government makes some hard decisions it will continue to fall in its regional importance," I stated.

The first three rows of the auditorium—where all the Government and Japanese officials were sitting—emptied out. I delivered the next part of my speech to their backs as they made, by Japanese standards, an unseemly dash for the exits. I briefly wondered if I had created a diplomatic incident but carried on for another ten minutes anyway, hammering home facts and figures to support my argument.

There was a deafening silence when I finished—no applause whatsoever. But the media clamour started soon after. We went to the Foreign Correspondents Club and the national and international press flocked around me. I got headlines on TV and in the major newspapers, including the Asia Edition of the *Financial Times*. At my next Board meeting I finally received a round of applause when I updated them on the Narita case.

After my speech in Tokyo, I told every member airline CEO to push what had been said at every opportunity. This would be their homework, their contribution. There would be no let up. The battle had begun and I was in the vanguard.

Lessons learned

It was not a bloody war but rather a cold one, a long silence with communication only through third parties. I went on hammering Narita at several international events. The pressure began to build on the airport as the financial community started to scrutinize its figures.

Bit by bit the airport started making some positive noises. I was happy to grant them a requested extended timeframe for discussions because IATA was now in the driving seat. And I fully understood the privatization issue was clouding matters. But I made it clear that I would give them time and keep silent as long as they gave me something in return: a reduction in charges and greater transparency going forward, which would include proper consultation with airport users.

The final, positive agreement was hammered out in a conference call with Masahiko Kurono, the new CEO of Narita Airport who had taken over shortly after the ACI event. I had a fluent Japanese speaker listen in for me who proved very useful, translating the various whispers on the other end of the line. Kurono and his colleagues never knew that I heard everything they were saying. But in the end, that didn't matter. It was an open and constructive conversation and was the first step on a journey towards the mutually beneficial relationship we have with Narita today. Kosaburo Morinaka, the new CEO, has been very cooperative and was particularly effective during the March 2011 earthquake, facilitating the necessary flights. The airport has changed a lot—as has Japanese aviation. New airports have been built and Haneda, Tokyo's other gateway, has finally been opened up to international traffic.

We are seeing a new breed of airport manager in Japan too. Outsiders with good experience of big corporations in the private sector such as Sumitomo and Toyota are coming in and running an airport as a business. Previously, Narita seemed to be a job for many high-level bureaucrats who were seeking a get-rich-quick scheme before retirement. There was absolutely no incentive for them to change the status quo. They just had to sit tight and wait for the golden handshake. Arrangements like the one at Narita explain the Japanese economy at large, which was stagnant for far too long.

The Narita case was a big gamble but it got the attention of the world's airports, governments and media. IATA had a new *modus operandi*. The member airlines also understood that a radical new approach was at play. We would shout, politely, and we would use facts and figures to make our point and cause public embarrassment where necessary.

The airline CEOs got behind this strategy quickly. They had taken up the Narita baton and were starting to have an impact in their domestic markets. Initially, it was just me making waves. But I had given the industry courage and no longer was I the only one shouting. It was not the voice of Giovanni that people heard but the voice of the industry.

It set the tone for the rest of my time at IATA. This would not be the association of the last 50 years. We would be a team of lions, not a flock of chickens. Jeff Poole, an experienced negotiator, was hired to head up a new user charges team. The time for quiet diplomats was over and some confidence began to return to the association. The idea of targets was not so daunting, the idea of leadership exciting.

The Taj Mahal with gates

Narita received so much negative publicity that it was becoming clear to all monopoly providers that new partnerships were needed; partnerships in which they responded to users' needs.

As a businessman and as the Director General of IATA I was well aware that airports needed to reward their capital. Business is business. But in too many cases, airport monopolies were taking too many liberties, running rings around phantom regulators and building monuments to their CEOs. These modern-days pharaohs were constructing their pyramids regardless of airline and passenger requirements.

I never called Toronto Pearson Airport a pyramid to my recollection. I did, however, use the word palace and variants thereof on many occasions. It was the "Palais de Versailles with boarding bridges", a "Taj Mahal with gates" and so on. Louis Turpen was the CEO, the former head of San Francisco Airport who had constructed an aviation museum there named in his honour. As CEO of Toronto Pearson, he had decided to build a huge new terminal. The airport did need a new terminal but I felt the decision on its scope was taken without adequate consultation with stakeholders or consideration of current events. The decision coincided with the Severe Acute Respiratory Syndrome (SARS) crisis, which was plunging most airlines into the red and some out of business altogether. Whilst some 15 airports reduced their landing fees to soften the blow, Toronto—despite being in the frontline as SARS spread—bucked the trend and increased its charges 29% to pay for its new cathedral.

I started my attack by publicly declaring that Canadian Minister of Transport David Collenette should "dramatically rethink the Canadian air policy agenda". The Greater Toronto Airports Authority responded by banning IATA from its premises and issued a written warning to airlines not to attend an IATA press conference due for 21 October 2003, which was going to make our feelings about Toronto Pearson clear. Both measures had no precedent in IATA history and both had no effect.

It was inconceivable to me that Canada, an efficient country, should have such high airport charges. The link between aviation and the economy is well documented and the damage to Canada caused by this high charges policy was huge. Moreover, the reaction to 9/11 in the United States had made the airport security process in that country very unpleasant. Near-neighbour Toronto had a real opportunity to grab market share from the

United States if it built an efficient passenger and airline-friendly airport.

Then CEO of Air Canada, Robert Milton, supported IATA's campaign as did the IATA Board. Robert was very active even though he had most to lose by picking a fight with one of his airline's principal hubs. His courage should be recognized as not many would have done the same. In his subsequent role as Chairman of IATA, he was instrumental in many of the association's successes and it was no surprise he transformed Air Canada. The fact that Air Canada's fortunes dipped again was largely due to the industry's fragile position and the airline's burdensome pension scheme, which had to hold reserves similar to a government corporation. It shows that an airline CEO should never relax. Recently, on a flight from Geneva to Montreal on Air Canada, a young cabin attendant recognized me and openly asked about the leadership of Calin Rovinescu, the CEO of Air Canada, and the reasons behind Air Canada downsizing. I just smiled and said, "He's working hard to keep your pension system alive."

It took a while to shift Toronto's position but I was comfortable with this having set a long-term strategy that had targeted new management at Toronto. In January 2004 Minister Collenette lost his position, the pressure from the IATA campaign combining nicely with other political developments. IATA continued to air its criticism of the airport management for another eight months. In August 2004 Louis Turpen resigned.

The only other way to force Toronto into submission would have involved some drastic curtailing of services, which would have affected passengers who had no need to be caught in the middle of our fight. The resignation of the two antagonists was the cleanest option and opened the path forward.

The new CEO, John Kaldeway, took a fresh look at the situation and we began a fruitful dialogue. In 2010, Toronto won an IATA Eagle Award, which recognized it as the Most Improved Airport. The GTAA battle has become a case study of how to win best practice from a partner.

One problem still remains with Canadian airports. No government has been strong enough yet to drop Canadian airport crown rents, a mere tax that fattens the federal coffers, but it is only a matter of time.

Airport privatization

Canadian crown rents are a privatization issue. Governments often want to privatize airports, not only generating cash from an initial sale but also charging an ongoing fee from the operator. Airport privatization became a major theme of my time at IATA. This is still ongoing and I don't imagine the issues surrounding it will go away any time soon. The issue here is not so much fighting our corner but ensuring the right framework is in place. You can't hand a monopoly to a private company.

Originally, IATA was very pro-privatization. Airports were largely owned by continually cash-strapped governments or government-run authorities and privatization held the promise of fresh investment, professional management and a desire for efficiency. For an airline, it was a chance to deal with a normal business partner rather than a bureaucratic mess.

IATA wasn't alone in its thinking. Privatization was once the magic word in Western society, the solution to many of life's woes and the only government model for new infrastructure financing. Actually, it's a very logical argument. Why should governments use public money to build something that would generate a good return on investment for a properly run business? Everybody benefits, including the end-user who would get a better service for less money.

But a visit to Madagascar in 2006 brought home the dogmatic nature of this philosophy. I had been invited there by Air Madagascar and the Minister of Transport, Roland Randriamampionona. The airline was struggling due to an overly competitive market, the machinations of governments in the region and poor infrastructure. A visit to the airport had been arranged and I had been told that a re-fencing project was almost complete thanks to a World Bank loan. This stopped cattle from roaming the airport, which presumably was a bigger worry to pilots than a bird strike. But one of the conditions of the World Bank loan was that the airport had to be privatized. This was completely inappropriate for a country without a stock market and the economic circumstances I saw around me.

Privatization has become a mantra in some circles. I understand—even agree—with the principle, but the practice has always been a let down because the policy is too often shoehorned into an inappropriate structure. The framework for privatizing an airport should be clear. The government needs to set a service level agreement that specifies deliverables such as waiting time for check-in, baggage delivery, re-investment levels and so forth. Benchmarking the efficiency of the airport as traffic increases is a must. Any failure to meet these signed levels of service should incur substantial penalties. A strong regulator should enforce the rules of the game, insist on transparency and be prepared to withdraw the concession.

It's difficult to see at first glance how it can all go so spectacularly wrong. Yet it always has. In July 2006, Grupo Ferrovial, inexperienced as an airport operator, bought the UK airport operator, BAA, for about $16 billion. This was an extraordinary price and sure to involve a crippling debt. The net result is failure. But penalties for this failure were set ridiculously low. From 2003–07, while airlines were reducing fares in real terms, BAA's charges went up 50%. They got away with an 86% hike for the 2007–12 period. Why? Airlines compete; airports do not.

The irony is that the concept of a regulator originates in the United Kingdom. But it seems incapable of providing one with any teeth. I coined the term "phantom regulator" specifically for the UK market although I've had to use it elsewhere since. I hope the UK Government doesn't mind. I do always try to give it credit for being the first to ruin this good idea. Regulators should continually challenge the concessionaire to be more efficient and any fines should really hurt. Repeated failure to meet service level agreements should mean the end of the concession.

To be fair, the BAA sell-off wasn't the worst. Ferrovial was inexperienced—but at least it wasn't a bank. In Australia in the 1990s, an important bank, Macquarie, started to buy up airports. Macquarie Airports' returns average 47%. It thinks this is okay because that's the level of return it gets on its other financial speculations. It is completely inappropriate benchmarking. It should be looking at the aviation value chain, not banks.

Auckland Airport is in a world of its own. I was in New Zealand in 2008 to meet with the Minister of Transport, Annette King, a very pleasant lady although very new to the job at that time. She was a former Minister of Health and I joked with her that the industry certainly needed a doctor. I shared with her some insights on the industry and, of course, mentioned that home carrier Air New Zealand was dogged by some very high user charges at its hub airport.

I gave Minister King all the relevant numbers, including margins made in other industries. The likes of Microsoft and IBM, for example, enjoyed returns averaging 20% to 40%. She was amazed when I told her that airlines average less than 1% and even a star performer like Singapore Airlines barely squeezes into double digits in a good year. In 2004, the pretax profit for Auckland Airport was 50%. I said I don't know who else can make that kind of money. The Mafia, perhaps, but despite being Italian, it wasn't a business with which I was familiar.

The next morning, all the national newspapers ran stories that explored this comparison between Auckland Airport and the Mafia. A parliamentary commission started an investigation and discovered the land was being valued like a shopping mall, giving rise to high profit expectations. Nothing much has been done though. Auckland Airport's pre-tax profits continue to impress if you're a shareholder and depress if you're an airline.

There is now a privatization problem looming with Brazil. With the soccer World Cup and the Olympics on the horizon, the government has sold off some of its main airports believing a private company could move faster and be more efficient in an infrastructure development process. I'm not sure of the reasoning there but anyway the auction strategy surpassed the government's expectations. The winning bids for Guarulhos, Viracopos and Brasilia airports reached $13.4 billion (BRL24.5 billion)—about five times the government's stipulated minimum. The crazy thing is the government will act as a regulator despite retaining a shareholder interest in the facilities. So it is in charge of deciding whether airlines should pay it a huge amount of money. We can guess at the answer. It is not the most promising business model from an airline point of view. How charges and services develop will need to be monitored closely.

There seemed to be a glimpse of light at the end of this privatization tunnel. India's regulator, the Airport Economic Regulatory Authority (AERA), established a single-till policy meaning all revenue, including commercial activity at an airport, is considered when setting user charges. So, the amount of money an airport makes in its shops from airline passengers goes toward offsetting the charges for the airlines. That seems fair to me.

Unfortunately, it has all gone spectacularly wrong in India with Delhi awarded a 340% price hike, basically because the government wants its slice of the cake. Other airports have put forward three-figure increases for approval. The former Aviation Minister Praful Patel was behind much of what is right about Indian aviation. Aside from AERA, he did a lot with Open Skies agreements and even steered a new terminal at New Delhi International Airport to completion in just 36 months, which must be something of a record for such a heavily bureaucratic industry in a heavily bureaucratic country. But he lacked the political support needed to see his policies through to conclusion and the merger between Air India and Indian Airlines has become a disaster. Kingfisher has been grounded for the time being and the most successful airline to date is Indigo. Jet's Airway's famous Chairman and founder, Naresh Goyal, is a leader with brilliant ideas and a very colourful character. He started from scratch and has had a very impressive career. At one point he was implementing the most elegant business class in Asia with the help of a famous Italian designer. He was so concerned about keeping the plans secret that all the mock-ups were set up in the garage of his wonderful London home. I think that shows how competitive airlines can be. Airports don't have to worry about things like this.

Anyway, the point is that it is very difficult for airlines to be effective when more than 10% of their revenue is spent on unrealistic infrastructure charges, which includes fees from both airports and air navigation service providers. During my time at the helm of IATA, user charges increased $10.1 billion while we secured cost savings in the region of $14.3 billion. Even so, airlines still pay their monopoly-owning partners in excess of $50 billion every year.

For now, I accept that airports cannot cover their costs simply through passenger-related shops and services, so airlines need to pay a fee. But charges must be transparent and fair. And in the future, airlines may not pay airports at all. Airports charge airlines for landing, for parking, for power and for just about anything else they can think of. In return airlines generate and bring airports the paying customers that make their huge returns possible. It seems a lopsided arrangement.

Overall, the situation with airports has improved though and there have been some notable successes, such as Geneva, where we have managed to help turn around what was once a very inefficient facility. Robert Deillon, CEO at Geneva Airport, has managed to oversee significant improvements in infrastructure with a limited impact on charges. We have also worked well with Montreal and Seoul-Incheon. IATA has done the lion's share of work in securing these improvements and the staff deserve a lot of credit. IATA's relationship with airports has been tense on occasion but it has steadily improved over the years. Airports now understand that IATA will continue to push them and there has been a definite shift towards partnership.

Stuck for space

One thing ownership doesn't change is the extent of airport capacity. The lack of it is a serious issue, particularly in Europe, although there are examples elsewhere such as Sao Paulo in Brazil or the New York system. Objections to new runways and extended terminals get plenty of media coverage while the arguments in favour are often an afterthought and portrayed as a minority opinion.

There are some very solid reasons why airports should be built or expanded. Basically, airports provide a huge boost to the economy, locally, regionally and globally. Asia-Pacific understands this and has invested heavily in new facilities that are forever winning "world's best" awards. Is it a coincidence that China is among the world's fastest growing economies and it has built 45 new airports during 2005–10 and plans another 52 by 2020? Or that Emirates Airline has become such a dominant force when Dubai International Airport has undergone massive development and the massive Dubai World Central Airport is being readied to become the world's largest airport serving 160 million passengers per annum? Look at it from the other angle: London Heathrow directly employs the best part of 220,000 people and the terrible decision to stop the third runway puts at risk the $49 billion worth of exports handled by Heathrow that go to non-EU countries. The number of destinations served by the airport has fallen by nearly 20% because of the lack of space, which means less passenger convenience and a lot less economic stimulus. London Gatwick now serves more destinations.

When I met with the UK Transport Minister, Philip Hammond, in 2010, I asked him why the government didn't have the courage to sign-up to a third runway at Heathrow. I explained how so many jobs, from manufacturing to hedge funds, had already been lost and that more would surely follow. He was very honest in his responses and said, politically-speaking, building a new runway was impossible in the foreseeable future. There has been a change in Minister since but the United Kingdom is still singing from the same hymn sheet.

Not building new runways should be impossible, politically-speaking. Even the environment angle has solid counter-arguments. For example, an extra runway allows greater flexibility in aircraft flight plans, potentially limiting the noise in particular locations.

And CO_2 emissions are being reduced on every single flight. Aircraft fuel efficiency has increased some 70% since the advent of the jet engine and airports have done a great job in improving rail links and using electric-powered ground support vehicles. Despite expansion, most airports have a smaller impact on the environment than they did previously.

CHAPTER FOUR

Raising the Profile

Using the media to
communicate strategy

Stop being shy

We shouldn't underestimate the external factors influencing aviation. Without the unwieldy government regulations or monopoly suppliers in the value chain, aviation would stand a better chance of sustainable profitability.

But we also have to be honest. Air transport has to take its share of the blame for these problems. The industry has been too slow, too shy, in voicing its complaints. It has lacked courage. Are we afraid of disturbing the sensitive souls of politicians? Or of ruining an airport CEO's afternoon tea? It doesn't matter if industry insiders know the facts. By definition, we are not the ones in charge of changing these external factors. Airlines must make their case publicly and make it loud and clear.

I became aware of this shyness while running Alitalia, but I was surprised to discover it was still the case when I joined IATA. The world had moved on but the industry and IATA's communications policy had not. Only local and trade press attended the IATA 2002 AGM in Shanghai. And there were no outside dignitaries. Effective communications is an important part of any business but for a trade association it is essential. An association must talk with its members, with the world. Politicians should hear what it is saying loud and clear. It would be a very poor industry body if it didn't do these things.

Despite my occasional strides into the headlines, early on in my leadership IATA didn't have any media strategy in place. I couldn't escape the feeling we were a ghost association, existing in our own aviation dimension, otherwise known as the trade press, but never crossing over into the real geopolitical world. Well, I intended to cross over and do some serious haunting.

At Alitalia, I understood the need for the airline to be injected into the national debate. I had a good communications team headed by Marco Zanichelli who helped me raise the airline's profile. When I travelled, we brought press along. Getting the Italian media on board was no big deal.

We were one of the biggest stories in town. But we were an international airline, so we needed an international presence. I set a challenge to get us into the *New York Times* and *Forbes*. We had a good story. Alitalia was number two in Europe, behind British Airways. We had transformed the company. The business world needed to understand how we did it and what we would do in the future. The challenge was met and eventually great articles appeared in the *New York Times* and *Forbes*. It had a very positive impact on Alitalia morale and our finances.

I was confident that IATA could, and should, be more famous.

A plane is not part of the deal

It was not necessarily a simple case of out with the old and in with the new when I shook up IATA's internal workings. Identifying employees who were ready for a step up was also part of the equation. Consideration had to be given to those who had the potential to play an effective role in the new strategy. And the net needed to be cast wide enough to include those not immediately visible to me.

A key position for the new IATA was Corporate Communications Director. It was evident at my first AGM in 2002 in Shanghai that corporate communications was a weak link. Airlines are exposed to a lot of media attention and I knew from my experience launching OPODO that telling people about your mission and targets was an essential factor in success. Communicating information is so important in today's world that a CEO cannot delegate the task to others. The CEO must be media-savvy, assertive, sure of facts and not afraid to respond. The press doesn't go for politeness. They like managers who are strong and articulate.

IATA's communication was none of these things. It wasn't saying anything—I guess because it didn't have anything to say. I see something similar in many airlines today. They lack the courage to stick with an effective strategy on a daily basis and only talk through the trade press. But that attitude is indicative of the industry's narrow thinking. It must aim higher—at the governments and the public who are aviation's partners and passengers. That involves talking to the general press and to TV and radio stations around the world. Trade press is for specific arguments, the general press is for communication in a broader context.

My first Director of Corporate Communications at IATA, William Gaillard, left just a few months after I joined to take up an exciting new opportunity with the European Football Association (UEFA). A head hunter was recruited to find William's replacement and we had some respectable candidates. But none fit the bill. While all had impressive biographies, they were used to large staff and large salaries. One candidate even had use of a private plane.

Around this time, SARS hit. Flights to and from China dropped 45% in June 2003 compared with June 2002. In May 2003, Cathay Pacific saw its passenger numbers fall 75%. Coming on the back of 9/11 and an economic downturn, it was an enormous blow. SARS was centred on Asia and so I turned to Tony Concil, who was based in our Tokyo country office. I asked Tony to move to Singapore and take leadership of the communications campaign. Tony had worked for All Nippon Airways for many years, was a fluent Japanese speaker and was immersed in Asian culture. He immediately showed a great sense of leadership and strength in his management style. I asked him to get more exposure with the general media but after a couple of months had no hesitation in making him the new Director of Corporate Communications. Soon enough we had built a team of people located around the world and Tony has continued to lead and show genuine team work. His appointment was a big surprise to the head hunter who had lined up many impressive names, but it sent a very positive and visible signal to the rest of the IATA staff.

Change, change, change

The circumstances surrounding the industry after 9/11 were compelling but it took a few months to develop my ideas about the story I wanted to tell. After Shanghai I asked the corporate communications department to detail the media coverage that had come out of the AGM. As I suspected, it was as if the event had never happened. There were some articles in the trade press about my clear message of change. But there was nothing in the mainstream press, apart from a couple of snippets in Geneva and Montreal about the size of a postage stamp. We couldn't honestly claim to have won so much as an inch of newsprint. We needed to do better. Like the estate agents' mantra of "location, location, location" we needed the whole world to know IATA and aviation was about change, change, change.

I managed to secure a slot with the BBC morning news as a way of testing the waters. Media is not as glamorous as many would think. I arrived at the central London studio early in the morning—before the sun was up. It wasn't a problem for me as I do not sleep much. The BBC studio, located deep inside the building, was taking advantage of new technology to be economical with space. It was like doing an interview in a closet. To make matters worse, the new technology wasn't working particularly well. I could barely hear the journalist who was broadcasting from another building. Still, it went well and they seemed happy with my unusual approach. I received a few calls of congratulations after the interview and I was happy that the industry was getting some coverage.

We had to have stories that would grab the headlines though. Narita was the first big one. Monopoly suppliers treating an industry as a cash cow and forcing prices up for consumers is always going to get air time and column inches. My shouting got me an interview with CNN while I was in Hong Kong shortly after my Tokyo trip. I could see that Tony was trying to prep me by asking questions in the car and in the elevator on the way to the studio. He didn't even let up in the Green Room. I was glad for the preparation. Rather than focusing on Narita, the interview was broad in scope, mostly covering security issues and the industry's financial situation.

After the interview I asked Tony how I had done. He hesitated briefly, perhaps not yet sure how honest he had to be with me, but then gave me a medium score.   I was a bit surprised but he followed up quickly with a suggestion—a short brief constantly updated to help keep track of the many numbers that we had to describe the industry's situation. The initial memo that he did evolved into a two-page bible that became a feature of my time at IATA. On those two sheets of paper, we put every number that gave a very clear and updated picture of what was happening in the industry or at a particular location. My job was to learn those facts and figures off by heart before I gave an interview. No easy task given how much those figures changed every month.

Building a communication strategy

Numbers are an important part of any media strategy. They help to tell the story. Sometimes my Italian passion led me to quote them out of context, but I feel that just made my presentations more vivid and memorable. Still, I was thankful for a communications team that kept the numbers—and my passion—in order. IATA began to gain credibility with the media for its open, factual approach and the concept of Giovanni "shouting politely" was born.

We built the media campaign around numbers that were both accurate and embarrassing for our opponents. It was easy at the outset with Narita and Toronto. And it didn't get much more difficult to be honest. After all, if I was arguing about something it was usually because I already knew the numbers were on our side. What we learned from those two early campaigns was that the industry had a compelling message and that there was an appetite in the press for what we had to say and the way that we said it. We got straight to the point and didn't fudge our words.

The airports provided the richest pickings—they were always the low hanging fruit. Wherever I went I could always drop in something about the airport's profits or the increase in charges. Eventually, airports started to wise-up and prepared some counter-arguments, but there was nothing that they could do to change the numbers.

At the behest of Narita, airports did manage to get Airports Council International (ACI) to adopt an anti-IATA resolution, however. ACI members agreed not to deal with IATA. I learned they were even exchanging notes, warning each other of an impending visit by the IATA Director General. Maybe they thought this would upset me. They thought wrong. I took it as a compliment. We were upsetting the apple cart and that is always the first step in genuine change. Quite by chance, only days after the ACI resolution, we concluded a major agreement on user charges with Copenhagen Airport. Their CEO, Niels Boserup, was heavily involved with ACI, but it was too far down the line for Copenhagen to pull out. I don't think they had any real appetite to do so anyway. To show the utter ineffectiveness of the ACI resolution, we promoted the agreement quite heavily in the media. The resolution was never invoked. It was silly and proved a complete waste of time.

These early successes energized the IATA team and I was full of ideas for accelerating the media campaign. But it's important not to lose focus. Don't just talk for the sake of talking. Change, change, change was the theme. Numbers were the evidence. Journalists started to respond to this approach. It gave them everything they required and they loved the candid, almost brutal approach. They realized that IATA was becoming a very different organization.

The transformation was underlined when the SARS crisis captured the world's attention in early 2003. We used a protracted media campaign to get airports to provide airlines with $100 million in cost savings through temporary relief in charges. Asking our partners in the value chain for urgent action on costs has become a standard request in crises affecting the industry. And we took leadership in working with the World Health Organization (WHO) to restore passenger confidence in flying. Quite honestly, we started the crisis naked. At first we knew nothing of the disease. But once we were sure that thermal scanners could detect the disease in its contagious form, we had a story. And we went out all guns blazing to make sure that everybody knew. I spoke at an ASEAN Prime Minister's conference in Bangkok to tell them to get behind scanner implementation without sending aviation an invoice. WHO backed up our message and people started flying again. It was still a bad time for the airlines but it could have been so much worse.

Internal and external confirmation

I wanted to reinforce IATA's new attitude to media and communication. Internally, I knew it would be important for the DG to explain the reasons for change, the way forward and the setting of targets. IATA established a new corporate newsletter, *In-Touch*, which was effectively prepared by Judith Gilson. This provides detailed information about new projects and initiatives so staff don't find out what IATA is doing by reading a press release. Staff should always be kept informed because it's a key component of motivation. I always attended key moments of any internal communication session as well. And I made a point to visit country offices whenever I was in their locality. Many of them are small— no more than a handful of staff—but I enjoyed explaining our strategy and reinforcing the need for constant two-way information flows with our members. This internal work was especially important for IATA, which is a geographically diverse organization. It created the corporate glue that kept the team together and working toward the same goals.

The external confirmation came through a successful re-launch of our magazine, *Airlines International*. A brilliant external consultant, Graham Newton, took over as Editor and effectively coordinated messaging with our corporate communications team. There was also a relatively minor logo change. Minor, that is, in terms of the image—it was a major step forward for the association. The old IATA brand was like an unwanted Christmas present, hidden away in a drawer or gathering dust on a shelf. IATA's new look, devised by Landor, the well-known marketing and design firm, was launched at the 60th AGM in Tokyo in 2005. Although largely unchanged from the 1947 original, the new logo incorporates a dynamic sky design to mirror the boldness of the new IATA. The approach is best summarized as "keep the trust, lose the dust". IATA was still the industry association but one imbued with new spirit.

Star of the small screen

My first AGM as Director General was in June 2003 in Washington, D.C. After a year at IATA, it was time to show that the association had received a DNA transfusion. It was forcing change internally and externally. And it would communicate that message to the world's media.

I put it simply and succinctly to the IATA Board prior to the Washington conference. "We always say that the world does not understand the airlines' problems. But we are not committed or willing to spread the message around. Why are we afraid? Our value proposition is good, we have reduced ticket prices 30% in the last few years. Our safety and labour productivity figures are equally impressive. It is time to have courage. My first AGM as CEO will be show time. I want CNN there to cover my State of the Industry address and to be involved in the event itself. Every other media outlet will be invited because airline CEOs will debate the crucial industry issues on stage. We will be on every TV news show and in every national newspaper."

There was silence in the room. From a closed door AGM to show time was probably too much for most of the Board. Leo Mullin, the CEO of Delta Air Lines who had hired me, was sitting next to me. After a few moments consideration, he said that this was a great idea. He could help with CNN and through him, we contacted Lou Dobbs. The flood gates opened and a deluge of ideas and other contacts followed.

The participants in the AGM CEO panel debate were Jeff Shane, at the time Under Secretary for Transportation in the United States, CK Cheong, Singapore Airlines CEO, Leo Mullin, Delta Airlines CEO, Jürgen Weber, Lufthansa CEO, and Herb Kelleher, Southwest CEO. That's a great line-up and they put on a great show. Herb, always a joker, was in wonderful form. He said he had prepared with great care for the event—his first ever IATA AGM—going as far as buying an expensive Italian suit to make me happy. I appreciated the gesture but as Herb fronted the world's most successful airline and was a business hero of mine, I wouldn't have cared if he was there in jeans and a T-shirt. That might have been more Herb's style anyway. He's a man who likes to have fun, inside and outside of work. We have spent many evenings together, Herb sipping a whisky while I stuck with Coke.

Lou Dobbs was a great anchor for the debate, but a little bit precious with his requirements. He certainly raised the profile of the event, for which I am grateful, but clearly a different approach, and a less demanding anchor, would be needed in future.

Starting with the next AGM in 2004 in Singapore we began to work with the BBC. The idea was to turn the AGM into the year's premier airline event, a place where everybody networked and the major issues were debated. Nik Gowing, BBC World's main news presenter, took to our vision instantly. Nik moderated every AGM until 2012, each year taking the debate to a higher level. We also had Aaron Heslehurst from the BBC who always livened up proceedings with his energy and effective style. He interviewed me on stage at my final AGM in Singapore and—to everyone's amusement—skillfully switched from showing some old photos of me during sports events, holding some guns, and my time at IATA.

I also developed a very good relationship with Richard Quest of CNN, who took over from Nik in 2012. Ever since we first crossed swords when I was at OPODO, he has led every interview with a very accusatory question. My Italian passion always rises to the bait but I think we both enjoyed this verbal jousting. Over time we became great friends. I have always admired his dedication to the industry. I remember a very cold, wet day toward the end of 2010, after the Yemen parcel bomb incident, when Richard decided to broadcast his prime time news show from our Security Conference (coincidentally running at the same time as the bomb incident). With an iPad and a satellite truck he broadcast an interview with me to the world from a very bleak, windy outdoor location. As I said, the media is not always as glamorous as you would expect.

I invested a lot of time with the media while at IATA and I don't regret a single moment. I built media into almost every trip and I worked hard to develop a good relationship with every member of the press. You cannot expect a story from every meeting but trust builds up over time. I even went as far as constructing a small TV studio in the Geneva office so we could be fast in reacting. My excellent CFO, Bob Hutt, was concerned about the cost, but in the end it was paid for by a TV company. It has increased IATA's visibility tremendously.

IATA averages a couple of press releases every month. On top of this I did TV and radio interviews and, depending on the subject matter, a number of related stories appear in the general press. Communication must be extensive but it must also be detailed and handled carefully. Being both tough and transparent is possible. Being readily available is essential. In February 2010, following a series of strikes and severe snow storms, I did an interview with Richard Quest outside my hotel in Berlin. It was late at night, freezing cold once again, and there was little cheer I could provide for passengers. But I answered every question and would have stood there for as long as Richard required.

Hold the front page

Of course, so prolific and many are the world's media outlets these days that you need to prioritize. Top of our wish list in the early days were the *Financial Times* and *The Economist*. These were the right publications to brandish our no-nonsense facts and figures style.

Before I confirmed Tony Concil as Director of Corporate Communications, he spent quite a lot of time building up IATA's presence in Europe. In the autumn of 2004, this diligent groundwork made it possible to invite *The Economist*'s Industry Editor, Iain Carson, to Geneva to see what the new IATA was all about. He spent a day with me and also met the key people. The following week, there was a Face Value column in *The Economist*. It covered the events in Tokyo, the internal reorganization and our aggressive approach to the future. I sent the article to all IATA employees as a symbol of the association's new-found relevance. I wanted them to know IATA was fast becoming the high-level, serious organization it needed to be. It would underline the speed, passion and commitment I was demanding of them.

Through the years I maintained a good understanding with *The Economist*, which was always supportive of our agenda—from Simplifying the Business to the Agenda for Freedom. When the new Editor, John Micklethwait, was appointed, we did a special briefing to its editorial board. My old boss Romano Prodi was a real fan of *The Economist* so it was a great honour to be in its boardroom, in between sessions with European Commission President, José Manual Barosso, government ministers and other captains of industry.

During my last months in office, I went back to the same boardroom. It was *déjà-vu* all over again, as the saying goes. We were talking about many of the same issues—technology, liberalization, high oil prices and world crises. I made the point that it was far from the same industry. The challenges kept on coming, but they hadn't killed us before and we were getting stronger all the time. We were making money at $110 a barrel when $25 a barrel was proving too much a decade ago. IATA taking some $55 billion in costs out of the industry had had an enormous effect.

The second publication that we put a lot of emphasis on was the *Financial Times*. I was in London once a month for the UK NATS Board Meeting. NATS is the United Kingdom's air traffic manager. It became a tradition for Tony Concil and me to use these occasions to meet with journalists. Kevin Done was the *FT* writer responsible for transport and we developed a routine of having breakfast with him at hotels in the Holborn area. We became great friends and Kevin later helped us with our Vision 2050 initiative. He wrote many interesting stories on IATA—including a key report on the 22.6% drop in air cargo in December 2008 that first symbolized the impact of the global economic slowdown.

Just as I had done at Alitalia with the *New York Times*, I challenged my people to get IATA on the front page of the *FT*. Some said that if airlines going bust couldn't do it then maybe we would have to murder an airport CEO. I was more positive. We eventually secured an interview with the *FT* on a trip to Brussels. We were trying to convince the European Commission to improve their regulation of airports. The reporter checked with the Commission and got a comment to the effect that "they were looking into it". It was a poor response to a strong argument.

The next day, back in Geneva, there was a stir in the corporate communications office. Calls were coming in on an *FT* story about regulation. We were all looking for the story in the Business Section and then under European news. Suddenly, somebody let out a gasp of surprise. We were on the front page! Persistence pays off.

It wasn't always industry issues that got IATA noticed. I've done a few profile pieces over the years and they always worked to our advantage. Ven Sreenivasan did an interview with me for the *Business Times* in Singapore. This was part of their "Raffles Conversation" series of exchanges with industry leaders. They eventually published a compilation of all the interviews. The book was put in every room at my favourite hotel in Singapore—The Raffles.

Raising IATA's profile in North America

IATA's presence in the United States was weak. Despite our headquarters in Montreal just across the border, we didn't have our finger on the US pulse. Not that there was any great mystery about US thinking in the first decade of the 21st century. It was always security. It didn't matter what else was going on—security was always priority number one, and understandably so given various terrorist outrages.

I made myself available at every opportunity—and visited frequently; simple hard work that brought a great result. Within a few years we went from obscurity to primetime on Fox TV, CNN and others. In turn that enhanced our ability to influence decisions. This became very clear from 2009 onwards in the progress that we made with the Department of Homeland Security (DHS). Secretary Janet Napolitano spearheaded a very different approach to security by the Obama Administration. She understood that security can only be more effective if a real partnership is built with the industry.

I was pleased with the change in attitude. Previous encounters with Secretary Napolitano's predecessors, Tom Ridge and Michael Chertoff, had been very disappointing. I couldn't get them to accept that the industry approach to safety, sharing information, was also applicable to security. They saw the matter as a national issue. Discussing potential policies with outsiders wasn't on their agenda.

After the foiled bomb plot on a Northwest flight to Detroit on Christmas Day 2009, I invited Secretary Napolitano to visit IATA in Geneva for a meeting with key industry CEOs, not to mention a more relaxing and very pleasant dinner. That she accepted so readily was a great sign of IATA's strength. I won't attribute our enhanced media presence with all of this success, but I have always believed that if you are read about in the papers, then you are seen as being relevant. Ask any would-be celebrity.

ICAO learned this lesson too. After the 2004 ICAO Assembly, I did a major press briefing as had become the norm. It got my picture in the papers and my meeting with the Canadian Minister of Transport a few days later was a lot more positive thanks to my photo staring up at him from the front page of the newspaper. The new Secretary General of ICAO, Raymond Benjamin, understood that I had the Minister's respect as soon as I walked into the room and he has been far more assertive with the media as a result. It's a different situation for him, of course, but he is using the media as much as possible. I'm happy to see ICAO get some attention. Their good work complements IATA's.

An eruption of truth

The power of TV really came home to me after the eruption of the Icelandic volcano in 2010, Eyjafjallajökull. I had just returned from a trip to Montreal and was immediately confronted with the news by my staff. For a few hours there seemed no obvious cause for alarm.

But during the night, I started to get phone calls in my capacity as a UK NATS board member. CEO Richard Deakin, who did a great job during the disruption, was updating me about potential problems. The volcano was his baptism of fire as he had been in the position only a couple of weeks. David McMillan, Eurocontrol Director General, and several European Ministers of Transport soon became involved in the discussions. A minor irritation was evolving into a full-blown crisis.

I was getting a lot of information from the TV news channels. Laid up with a terrible cold, the embarrassing mess unfolding hour by hour just made my temperature worse. Millions of passengers were stranded. There was no action from the European Commission. And the skies were wonderfully clear and blue.

We had a pre-scheduled meeting with a Paris media association on 19 April, five days after the initial eruption. It was meant to be a very friendly breakfast chat in the historic Café Procop in Paris. Of course, there were no flights operating. And to add insult to injury, the French railways were on strike. So I drove to Paris with Tony Concil and along the way we plotted to make some noise at the event.

We contacted CNN and the BBC to arrange interviews for the morning of 19 April, starting at 6am. I still had a terrible cold, so doing the first broadcast for CNN from a rooftop overlooking the Champs Elysées was a challenge. But I summoned up the energy and began my polite shouting. Next was the BBC over the phone, followed by five other interviews. We managed to cover the major European morning news shows before the Paris breakfast even began. And as I began my speech there, Tony was busy alerting the other press to what we were saying. Thanks to my good friend in Iceland, Sigurdur Helgason, my information was more accurate than that supplied by the air traffic controllers. He could see the volcano from his house in the country. The sedate Café Procop was transformed. By the time we finished there were TV crews practically hanging from the chandeliers. One even chased me down the street and we ended up with an impromptu interview in front of the Ritz Hotel.

I was shouting that we needed leadership. European Ministers took days just to agree a conference call, which was a complete failure to lead. And decisions were being based on theory. Every proper test showed that the ash either wasn't there or wasn't there in sufficient density to cause any safety issues. Closing Europe's airspace was costing the regional economy billions and inconveniencing passengers around the world. It was the greatest European embarrassment that I have ever seen and a clear indication of the lack of leadership.

The new European Commissioner for Transport, Siim Kallas, wasn't happy with me. But somebody had to say it. It was the truth. Fortunately, the relationship with Commissioner Kallas improved after we found common ground on some Single European Sky issues at the Davos summit in early 2011. We've since become good friends.

But the media lesson from my road trip was clear. I drove thousands of kilometres in two days to deliver the airline message in Paris, Brussels and Berlin. Given that over 400 journalists now attend our AGM and over 100 visit Geneva for the Global Media Day, it is fair to say the communication efforts proved worthwhile.

Speaking clearly

As Director General of IATA I gave many speeches. At the beginning it wasn't easy. English is not my first language. I also had to get used to standing in front of an audience of a thousand people and telling the brutal truth—even if it embarrassed my hosts.

But after Narita, the reality started to dawn on me. The governments, airports and other stakeholders listening were more scared than I was. They knew their guilty business secrets were about to become public knowledge.

When it comes to speeches, I first outline the broad message to my team and indicate how far I may wish to go in exploding some established practices. It is essential to make an impression. If you are going to do an event, do it properly, so that people remember. Using the numerous tools now available from Power Point to videos helps to capture attention. But they must be used wisely. I see little value in endless slides of charts and text-heavy bullet points, which you simply repeat in your speech. They are boring and they don't tell a story.

But an image can make a big impression while you're hammering home the facts. It underlines the central point and cements your argument in the audience's mind. We had a very talented young designer at IATA, Richard McCausland. He developed a specific style to illustrate my speeches that became a trademark of my presentations. We created some very memorable moments together.

A regular feature of my AGM state of the industry address was the Wall of Shame. On big slides we put up the names of industry partners that were taking advantage of their monopoly position. It is a serious point but we balanced this by having some fun at their expense. In 2010, we were having some major problems with the global distribution systems, the companies that provide flight information to travel agents. I wanted to highlight this at the AGM and inserted the term "leeches" into my speech. I called it as I saw it—they were sucking the lifeblood of airlines. When it came to illustrating this section, Richard had some trouble. He was trying to be polite. The initial image was of leeches crawling on a throat. But I wanted the extra step, the indelible mark—I wanted to see blood. And when I had that, I also got the GDS names on the slide, to be sure there was no doubt. I admit the IATA Corporate Secretary, Tom Windmuller, and the IATA General Counsel, Gary Doernhoefer, did caution me to use a more considered approach, but I decided to ignore their suggestion. The blood-soaked leeches with GDS names ended up being the most memorable slide of the presentation. It got a long round of applause. I received the "Tell it like it is" award with a personal note from one of the industry's great communicators—Herb Kelleher, famous for his development of Southwest Airlines and an old friend from my Alitalia days. To me that was a great honour.

Of course, I got some very strong letters of objection from the GDSs, but fortunately IATA's successes in the court battles that were going on at the time rendered their tantrums mute. In a case against Sabre, the court ruled that IATA's PaxIS product did not infringe any rights Sabre had claimed. PaxIS (Passenger Intelligence Services) was essentially a market intelligence database. Airlines could see travel trends and adjust their strategy accordingly. The GDSs had a similar data product. We were processing our member's information to create and sell a market information product and analytical web tool a lot cheaper than the GDSs which had more than a 90% margin. We also avoided liability for material damages claimed by Amadeus and IATA has a positive preliminary decision in the case against Travelport. Antitrust litigation brought by American Airlines against Sabre was recently settled with an undisclosed amount of compensation paid by Sabre. The US Department of Justice Antitrust Division is also investigating GDS behavior for compliance with the antitrust laws.

If you have fun with speeches you're far more likely to create a memorable impression. I remember when I addressed the European Aviation Club in Brussels in 2004. I wanted to give Europe a wake-up call that change was essential. It was about the time that the European Commission had introduced draconian laws for compensating passengers for delays and cancellations. Let's be clear about this: fines won't stop it snowing, huge compensation deals won't stop volcanoes erupting, and providing care for passengers should surely start with enough runways and airspace.

Anyway, as a publicity stunt, Commission officials had been handing out leaflets in the airports to inform passengers of their rights—which was simply digging a deeper hole. So when I went to make a speech in their home territory, I prepared my own leaflets to publicize the embarrassing lack of leadership on the continent. We outlined $8 billion in damages that Europe's power-hungry bureaucrats were doing to the industry. The leaflets were handed out as I was talking. It did not make me popular in the Commission's corridors, but it delivered a strong message and many saw the humour in it.

Some of my speeches also developed a brand beyond the graphics. When we were working on my AGM speech for 2006 in Paris, I was looking for a way to express the frustration that the industry was feeling as a result of inefficient airports and suppliers. I wanted a one-word retort and the only one that would do was from my native language: *basta* (enough). When I shouted it out at the AGM, it captured the mood of the industry perfectly. There was a great round of applause. People understood the message…or so I thought.

Apparently the Chinese translators couldn't work out why even an Italian would mention "pasta" at a crucial point in the speech. Others came up afterwards to shake my hand but whispered calling the airports "bastards" was a bit blunt and strong even for me. I've been very careful how I say the word ever since. But it became a trademark of my AGM speeches from then on and I even received a silver "basta" ornament at my last AGM in Singapore in 2011. I don't use my "basta's" gratuitously, so when I say it, the industry knows I mean it. And at the end of the day, that is what communications is all about.

CHAPTER FIVE
Getting Technical

Simplifying the Business and the role
of technology

Ambitious undertakings

Of course, in this game you have to do more than just talk the talk…you need to walk the walk. In business speak, you have to deliver. Trouble was, the air transport industry was used to limping along from one crisis to the next. IATA needed to provide it with a crutch.

In the end we did more than that. We provided the platform that has enabled the industry to make money despite the oil price averaging a whopping $110 a barrel. That platform is known as Simplifying the Business and it was originally centred on a plan to eliminate the paper ticket, saving airlines about $9 for every single seat they sold.

At a meeting at Heathrow chaired by BA CEO, Rod Eddington, the idea of e-ticketing (ET) was first aired. It was working well on the few carriers that were using it and it would give legacy airlines a chance to close the gap with low-cost carriers. Although its use was limited there was support for the idea, particularly from Robert Milton at Air Canada and Leo van Wyck of KLM.

We began to brainstorm the concept internally at IATA. A few of the more extreme ideas got thrown out but we could see how others—common use self-service check-in (CUSS) and bar-coded boarding passes (BCBP), for example—were complementary. I also asked Tom Murphy, my Senior Vice President, to carefully analyze the role of the Internet. He was a former British Airways manager and had great knowledge of distribution. In any case, my OPODO experience had taught me that the Internet was going to be vital to a future distribution system.

I first mentioned our work to the IATA Board in late 2003. We were enduring a downbeat meeting with plenty of moaning about the low-cost carriers, which were stealing a sizable part of the legacy carriers' market at the time. I needed to raise the energy levels, so wasted no time in playing my trump card. I told the Board there was a program in preparation that would replicate the LCC model by rebuilding the elemental processes of aviation.

Isao Kaneko, CEO of JAL, looked astonished, as did some of the other Board members. Their surprise was a good sign. It meant some fresh thinking was finally being introduced to aviation debates. Milton and van Wyck were, of course, very supportive.

E-ticketing wasn't just about the ticket though. The StB program had identified ways to take paper out of the entire distribution chain. In addition to the move to an e-ticket, StB would also include projects in CUSS, BCBP, radio frequency identification (RFID) and e-freight. The airlines would save billions. And it was a classic win–win because it would touch the passenger too. The 2 billion-plus travellers would get a better, harmonized service making the airport process more efficient whether they were in the United States, Europe, Asia or Africa.

Although by 2004 the Internet was firmly established and airline websites were becoming a lot slicker, the airline business model was still centred on two building blocks: the 70,000-strong travel agency distribution system, through which airlines sell their tickets; and interlining, which enables passengers to fly with multiple carriers on a single ticket.

This complex system involves over $300 billion per year, moving between passengers, agents and airlines. The link between them all was the paper ticket. Over time this had evolved into a neutral document that was recognized by all airlines around the world. In practice, it was aviation's currency. Each ticket had to be distributed securely, was stored in safes, and had a unique identifier that allowed the ticket to be tracked through its entire lifecycle.

The paper ticket made it relatively straightforward for one airline to issue tickets on another airline, known as interlining. For example, a passenger would get a ticket that enabled them to fly from London to New York on British Airways and then on to Miami on American Airlines. The passenger would hand each airline an individual coupon, or ticket, when checking-in for each flight. The airline would then use that coupon as the proof of carriage and claim its money from the airline who first issued the ticket. A very simple concept, no doubt, but in practice it was a complex and long-winded process. Although airlines just needed to sign an interline agreement and agree to the terms for transferring the monies—usually through IATA's settlement systems—over time it became extremely costly to administer.

It took armies of people to manage these mountains of paper. Travel agents gave paper tickets to passengers. Passengers gave them to check-in staff. Those staff tore off one ticket coupon at a time, and if the coupon had been sold on the other side of the world, it was then sent thousands of miles back again to be processed. The system was also far from foolproof. Missing coupons were an everyday occurrence.

The key difficulty was that to eliminate the paper mountain the whole industry needed to move together. And we had to be quick too. Managing paper and electronic tickets at the same time would be more costly than just keeping the paper. Interline ET (IET) was another difficult proposition. Each airline needed to establish an electronic connection with every one of its interline partners, which meant a full technical interface costing up to $10,000 each time. Not only did this cost mount up as interline agreements are fairly commonplace—some airlines have as many as 200—but for some agreements, which handled just a few tickets a month, the price couldn't be defended. Add in the fact that the time to implement a full electronic interface between two airlines could be up to four months and you had some very tough decisions on your hands. It's fair to say that in the beginning, 100% IET seemed completely unrealistic.

But if airlines decided not to implement IET with their partners, in effect cutting each other off, a large percentage of passenger journeys would either stop being offered or would need to be ticketed separately. That would be a major problem for a project proposing to improve customer service.

Time for a revolution

Despite all these challenges, I was confident of the end goal. Preparing the ET project took several months but in May 2004 it was ready to roll. I had discussed the topic with a raft of airline CEOs ahead of the Board meeting that would ratify the project. While they applauded the potential savings it was obvious that many viewed ET as a nice theory— and nothing more. It was a minor concern for me though. In essence, everyone agreed that ET was a great idea. That was all I needed. It would be difficult to backtrack from that simple assertion. So, at the Board meeting, once we were all smiles around the table, I spelled out the final component. The project needed a deadline. We had to say exactly when IATA would cease distributing neutral paper tickets.

Suddenly, the atmosphere changed. The Board meeting became extremely tense. Smaller airlines were naturally reluctant to embrace such radical change in a tight timeframe. For instance, many airlines in Africa were totally unprepared, lacking both the knowledge to implement the new system and the financial means to fund it. But IATA's remit had changed. I assured these airlines that we were no longer a club for major airlines. I told them they could count on our support, including free of charge consultancy services and expert resources. These would be paid for by our rapidly improving commercial section.

More surprisingly, an unexpected number of large airlines did not want to move forward so quickly, notably Japan Airlines, Air India, Emirates and Virgin Atlantic. I received many letters trying to delay the process. Reasons varied, and certainly they were equally concerned about making big investments, but a crucial factor was the arrangements they had with the distribution channels. This was a project with huge consequences for the distribution chain, including fees payable to the existing distribution system. Identifying a suitable date—in fact any date—for the project deadline turned out to be a tough negotiation. More than once I had to resort to one of my preferred taglines: "No target, no business". Things were getting heated.

Fortunately, Robert Milton, Air Canada CEO, was once again a strong supporter of my stance. With him fighting by my side I was able to seal an end-2007 target for the ET initiative. To be honest, I think we secured an agreement because more than a few members thought the target would slip, perhaps even be forgotten about. Because of this, the meeting ended pleasantly with everybody joking about being rid of the paper mountain.

About a month later, I made sure the doubters didn't find it so funny any more. We put out an advisory to all our members that delays wouldn't be tolerated. Airlines that weren't 100% ET by end-2007 would no longer feature in the IATA Billing and Settlement Plan, the back-end financial network. They would effectively be cut off from the industry. And in case they doubted my word, I put in a termination date on all our contracts with the paper suppliers. There would be no way to print a ticket.

False dawn

Formal Board approval was a great start but I had to roll my sleeves up and get the right team in place to ensure our tough target would be met. It needed a certain skillset, an ability to dangle carrots as well as wield sticks. And technical understanding had to be coupled with a thorough knowledge of the regulatory and business processes involved.

I had already started head-hunting with the assistance of Michael Bell from Spencer Stuart, an executive recruitment firm. Michael was the most experienced head hunter in aviation and had recruited me to IATA. We needed to find the right man to lead the team. After an extensive search, I hired a US national whose experience included top positions in the distribution world. His biography ticked all the right boxes and he interviewed well.

But it wasn't the right decision. It's hard to pinpoint exactly when I started to worry, but from the start I had an instinct that he didn't quite fit in. Too much bluster, not enough drive. While my sleeves were rolled up, he seemed to be idly pulling his cuffs straight. It just goes to show that a good résumé isn't enough. You have to get past the technical skills to see if the person has passion. I'm a facts and figures man, not one for therapy sessions, but the passion to deliver on a good résumé is as important as the résumé itself.

After a few months in the job, our new recruit had spearheaded a strategy focusing on an arbitrary selection of a few major airlines. It smacked of the big boys club I had worked so hard to disband. We learned very little from this initiative and achieved no tangible results. During IATA's annual top management meeting in Montreux, Switzerland, I fired him. Several members of the team felt he should be given more time but I just knew I had made a mistake in recruiting him. He hadn't shown the sense of urgency or the leadership necessary to build the consensus that this job required. Moreover, he seemed to be more supportive of those airlines that did not want to change fast enough. In any case, the fairest thing for all concerned was to end the relationship as quickly as possible.

And it had to be done for the industry's sake too. Airlines were bleeding money and this was no time to bed in somebody who may have never made the grade anyway. It was essential not to compound the initial mistake of hiring him by failing to recognize the error and then failing to act. Mistakes, wrong decisions—they are a part of life and the business experience. The only thing to be afraid of is not having the courage to admit to them and putting them right with all possible speed.

But although I acted swiftly it was still a few months wasted. The end-2007 deadline didn't allow room for such a slow start and the project was seriously off track. And of course, we were now missing a project leader. I knew we couldn't afford another mistake so decided to abandon the classic head-hunting process. Instead, as with corporate communications, I turned inward and made a careful assessment of our in-house resources, focusing on the recently recruited managers.

I identified the Director of IATA's Industry and Financial Services, Philippe Bruyère, freshly arrived at IATA from Crédit Suisse. While he had no specific experience in distribution, he came from a strong financial background. The complexities of how the money moved around the distribution chain wouldn't be lost on him. Importantly, he understood process and he understood the need for speed and leadership. The appointment of Philippe as the head of the StB project created quite a stir within the organization. He was young and taking over from a man who had been a CEO in his role prior to IATA. Many thought it was another crazy Giovanni idea. But it worked. It was further positive reinforcement that there were great opportunities for personal development. I asked Philippe to build on this impetus. He had to develop a strategy and put a team together within ten days. I gave him free rein—he could choose from the best managers available at IATA to help him.

Inspired by authors such as John Kotter and his eight steps of change, Philippe devised a 100-day strategy. His approach was precise and covered all the essential points. The premise was simple: the only way to achieve a revolution was to mobilize the entire industry. This meant that every single airline (500-plus), every single travel agency (70,000-plus), every single airport (1,600-plus), not to mention every single one of the 2.4 billion people who travel by air, would need to embrace proactively the transition from paper ticket to ET.

Creating the networks

Easier said than done, of course. Airlines were cutting staff to keep costs down so there was little in the way of human resources to make the internal changes. They were also squeezing travel agent commissions due to the tight economic conditions, so bringing these two parties together for a common cause required some delicate negotiations.

Setting up internal and external networks provided the framework to take the process forward. The external network was based on a concept of accountability. If someone is made personally accountable for an objective, they will take actions to achieve it, including mobilizing their staff as well as their suppliers and customers. This creates a virtuous circle involving more and more people. By March 2005, letters were flying out of the IATA head-office tasking some 500 airline CEOs to appoint an StB Champion from their senior management ranks and an e-ticketing contact.

One member of the IATA ET core team was assigned to each world region to support this external network. They would research their region's specific ET challenges and train an IATA StB representative in each country on how to help their local airlines implement solutions. This empowerment model gave the local IATA people the tools, information and support necessary to push their airlines to make progress. In turn, it provided IATA with some tough young motivated managers without whom StB wouldn't haven't been so successful. The IATA country and regional project support teams were required to contact all 400 BSP-using airlines each time we conducted a survey on capability and plans—which we did six times during the project. So there were about 2,400 meetings on ET alone. In addition, the StB Steering Group was carrying on with its work, with ET usually taking up about half of its meetings. My scheduled appointments with airline CEOs were ET-centric too. I had about 30 ET briefings prepared for me so I could push CEOs harder.

At any point, the StB Champion at an airline could call the ET regional expert in the IATA core team and get an immediate answer to a question. They could even request a mission where the ET expert would fly in for a few days and provide local support.

The external network needed feeding with knowledge, expertise and coordination. That's where the internal network came in. At its centre was Philippe who would have to translate strategy into action. He had chosen some good people. Bryan Wilson, an expert in IT systems and processes and a former top manager at SITA, joined the IATA StB team as ET Project Director. In this capacity, Bryan led the project team of experts and was responsible for identifying and overcoming technical, legal and political obstacles that posed a risk to 100% ET. In each country there was an IATA StB representative and in each regional office there was an StB Regional Program Manager. Each person took on this role in addition to their daily jobs and was given accountabilities and targets along with the necessary incentives. Eventually, the IATA StB team reached 80 people covering over 90 countries.

We had established a methodology that formed the foundation not just for ET but for all StB projects. Essentially this involved measuring progress through data. The airline CEOs were an important part of the relationship and they were constantly informed of ET progress. So while there was a global agenda, there was very much a focus on local implementation. You have to understand the reality on the ground.

That's really what the StB Champion and local IATA contact was all about. We began a campaign to raise awareness and build the relationship between these "on-the-ground" contacts. It was the IATA representative's job to present on the ET project and its objectives, raise the airline's awareness on what action needed to take place and by when, and then ask the airline champion for their formal commitment to the action plan. Within four weeks of the project's announcement, they had been trained to do this and answer any possible questions. Within six weeks, over 300 meetings had been held across the world on e-ticketing. Reports were flying in to Geneva. Each report stated the date of the meeting, the people in attendance, the current status of ET implementation at the airline, and the plan to achieve the 100% vision. For the first time, there was information on the state of the industry in terms of ET.

That was the good news. The bad news was the information showed all too clearly how ill-equipped the industry was to adopt ET. Every week I met with the team for an update, I often had to take responsibility for calling up an airline CEO to push them harder.

Progress initially was painfully slow and out of IATA's hands. Internally, ET cut across airline departments and the airline StB Champion had to break down silos. Commercial people weren't used to talking to operational people and they didn't have much to do with the technical guys either. I could only sympathize. It reminded me of my first months at IATA.

But eventually things started to happen. I had followed up personally with many airline CEOs to support the ET process. I also went directly to governments to tell them to prepare to change the law. Many countries required a paper document for fiscal or visa purposes, so they had to switch to accepting an e-format. And to counteract the economic constraints, IATA was providing all the necessary financial resources to support its member airlines. In my speeches I started to emphasize that "no one gets left behind".

ET started to spread like a virus, starting with IATA and stretching through its representatives to the airline StB Champions and on to the various airline departments. ET fever was hitting the industry. Despite all the challenges, the first target of 40% ET was achieved ahead of schedule in November 2005.

Colour by numbers

We had to shock people to get there though. Prior to the June 2005 Tokyo AGM, the StB team produced a series of ET reports for airline CEOs. Each report was customized by airline and handed out individually to the CEOs at the AGM. They showed the results of that first campaign—in effect providing feedback to the airline CEO on their own management of the ET campaign.

The individual report explicitly presented the airline's status on e-ticketing based on the available data. A simple colour scheme was adopted. Red airlines were those with no plan to meet the target; orange were those with a plan but still no ET capability; yellow were ET-capable; green were interline ET-capable; and platinum were 100% ET-capable in all aspects.

At the 2005 AGM there were no platinum airlines at all, while the green or yellow carriers were the better resourced ones. Many airlines were still orange or red. In total, 245 airlines had still never issued an electronic ticket. The reports were short, structured to be easy to read and they proved very effective. They shocked the CEOs. It was just as I had planned because we had reached a stage where the project needed an injection of speed and a greater sense of inclusion. Far too many CEOs were still just talking the talk and they had to be embarrassed into taking action. The CEOs had not just heard speeches on how ET would become a reality; they had all given speeches on how ET would become a reality. And here in front of them were reports stating that on current trends they had no hope of making the target. In addition, the reports included a shopping list of challenges to overcome. This information, backed up by industry data on the potential revenue loss if the airline did not meet the target, added to the pressure.

Perhaps it was a bit harsh but these unsubtle hints did the trick. The CEOs started to realize that to meet the 100% target required action—

urgent action—from them. Armed with the reports, they went back to their management teams demanding results. In fact, many didn't wait until they arrived back in their home country. I was delighted to see quite a few making frantic calls on their mobile phones immediately after receiving the report. Showing them the red card improved their game no end.

Phone a friend

To reach our goal, airlines needed technical expertise and regular help. Hundreds of ET projects were going on around the world and the main suppliers of technical help were stretched to the limit. ET expertise was in short supply.

IATA had to help but it wasn't straightforward. We had to walk the tightrope between staying out of commercial disputes and making sure the entire industry made the transition. Aside from all the other initiatives, two new self-engagement tools were launched. The aim was to bring transaction costs down and to speed up the ET implementation process. The ET Matchmaker was an airline tool that allowed one airline to contact a counterpart in the network and ask them if they wanted to interline, how they wanted to proceed and when they wanted to begin the work. Requests were either accepted or rejected/ignored. If accepted, implementation and follow-up meetings were held. If rejected or ignored, the airline knew it had to make other plans. The second tool, the General Business Requirement (GBR) Generator, enabled airlines that had agreed to interline to establish their electronic terms quickly.

These two initiatives brought the average interline implementation time down from the previous best of four months to just two weeks. By the end of 2006, IATA was projecting that over 80% of current interline journeys would be ticketed by the deadline, with the remainder being easily tackled with minimum inconvenience to the customer. And that was a conservative estimate.

All we had done really was identify the problems quickly. Then we brought in experts to solve the problems, translate the solutions into something non-experts could apply and finally drive the implementation.

It didn't mean we were home and dry though. The sheer amount of work was putting airlines under incredible pressure. By early 2007, the strains of the tight deadline were becoming more visible as airlines struggled to complete 100% ET. Many were genuinely doing their best but for some, it was a convenient excuse. It was becoming clear that a few airlines would have to be dragged into the modern, paperless world kicking and screaming.

We quickly identified another opportunity for assistance. Those airlines nearing 100% ET now had under-utilized experts. So why not ask an advanced airline to send one of their experts to an airline that needed the expertise? An ET buddy system. Initially, this was done between airlines that were part of the same alliance, but that soon became a pleasantry we neither needed nor could afford. Soon enough, experts were flying around the world to offer help wherever it was required—a real example of industry cooperation. Titus Naikuni, CEO of Kenya Airways, in particular deserves some praise. He was instrumental in helping several African carriers.

Not all problems could be solved on an individual buddy basis. So IATA also sponsored regional workshops where airlines, vendors and experts would come together to share their progress and problems, learn about solutions and agree on how they would work together in an electronic world.

Airports without any kind of electronic infrastructure were an especially tricky conundrum and the source of both amusement and bemusement at the regional workshops. No electricity at all seemed a reasonable excuse for failing to implement ET. Not for the StB team though. Kenya Airways implemented ET at Lamu Island, a small Kenyan dirt airstrip off the coast that had no power. The loadsheet was brought out to the airport by a check-in agent who took the boat from the mainland town before each flight. A video of the story was shown at the 2007 Vancouver AGM and put to shame airlines who still claimed that global ET was impossible.

Eliminating paper tickets

That final year, we had to overcome various problems from the small to the large. I hit the road to highlight the importance of meeting the target and to offer any assistance necessary to airlines in difficulty.

Egyptair was facing serious issues because its old, legacy systems couldn't cope with ET and major financial investments were required. It was only due to the leadership of the CEO, Atef Abdel Hamid, that Egyptair got on board before the final furlong. Air India was stuck in a similar situation, something of a surprise in a country that is the home to many of the world's biggest IT companies. Malaysian Airlines was another example and, again, thanks to the commitment and vision of its CEO, Idris Jala, it was able to meet the deadline.

These airlines really just needed a massive dose of motivation to take them over the line. Others had more deep-seated problems. MIAT, the airline of Mongolia, is a case in point. Its CEO, Orkhon Tseyen-Oidov, asked for my personal help. Of course, I responded positively and a month later, in March 2007, I arrived in a very cold Ulan Bator. The Mongolian capital is a strange but wonderful place. It is surrounded by stunning natural scenery but has a coal power station planted right in the middle of a humble, rudimentary city. It's not exactly environmentally-friendly, but it gives the city more grandeur than you would expect.

At MIAT headquarters, a modern building in the airport area, the CEO introduced me to his team. The managers were all very young. As ever, I had prepared for the meeting. I took out my notes expecting that their first request would be an extension of the deadline. This was the usual demand of an airline facing difficulties. Instead, they had very precise questions as to how to reach the targets from a business and technical viewpoint. I was given a very accurate presentation on the ET program that they were currently working on. I was surprised but very impressed and promised I would help them. In truth, I only had to make one call—to the CEO of SITA, Francesco Violante. SITA run many of aviation's background IT systems. As ever, my friend Francesco was very responsive and gave them the assistance they needed. MIAT made the deadline.

To extend or not to extend

By February 2007, forecasts for the end-of-year ET compliance figure were running at around 90%. An amazing achievement for sure, but still not good enough.

At the same time, letters from stressed CEOs started arriving at IATA. They pleaded for an extension to the deadline. Russian carriers, which had just received legal approval to issue their first ET after years of government delays, now had only a few months to make a journey that other airlines had taken years to complete. I had discussed this problem with my good friends, Transport Minister Igor Levitin and the Aeroflot CEO Valery Okulov, on a number of occasions. While they had understood the concept from the start, some senior cabinet officials had stubbornly insisted a paper ticket was a fiscal necessity and paper ticket distribution was handled by an unreliable outside agency. IATA strongly supported the Minister Levitin and our staff paid dearly for this support. Our Moscow office was raided by the police at gun point. Two employees ended up in hospital. Our country manager, Dimitri Shamraev, behaved impeccably and the Swiss Ambassador to the United Nations in Geneva, Dante Martinelli, also acted very effectively on our behalf. In the end Minister Levitin finally won out just a few months before deadline.

Other carriers were asking for a delay to e-ticketing for more selfish reasons. JAL, for example, was uncomfortable with a global model and was lobbying smaller Pacific carriers to ask for an extension. And Virgin Atlantic just seemed to be reluctant to join in on an industry initiative. The brand has a trendy, innovative image but in this case the reality was somewhat different and their CEO, Steve Ridgway, had to be persuaded by CS Chew of Singapore Airlines (SQ). It probably isn't a coincidence that SQ was a major shareholder in Virgin.

In a confidential report prepared for me, the StB team recommended that a four-month extension of the deadline should be enough to meet the target. Six months was the outside figure and anything more than that would be a danger to the project in terms of lost momentum. There were also cost implications for those airlines that had made the deadline. Having to maintain paper relations with a few stragglers was, in effect, a financial penalty for doing the work on time. That didn't seem fair.

The 2007 Vancouver AGM was now fast approaching where we would be reporting, in a transparent manner, the ET positions of all IATA members. The decision over the extension was weighing heavily on my mind and I ordered preparations for a formal vote on the matter at the AGM, printing the ballot papers and ordering the voting boxes. A proper vote like this had never arisen in the 60 years of IATA's history. But it showed how important this was. We had come a long way since 2004 and managing the extra 5% to 6% paper tickets gap was so frustrating. I desperately wanted to keep to our timeframe even though only a few years before most of our members and partners were all betting on the paper ticket having a long and happy life.

When the first AGM delegates arrived in Vancouver, it was clear that the supporters for a deadline extension intended to be very vocal. It wasn't all self-pitying diatribes. Like the Russians, some were genuinely handcuffed by government legislation that insisted on a needlessly cumbersome, bureaucratic paper trail. Why governments resist change and innovation, even when the evidence in favour is indisputable, is one of life's great mysteries. Delays in changing the regulatory framework are not measured in months or years, but in decades.

Anyway, I worked on a plan with the IATA Board Chairman, CS Chew of Singapore Airlines, and the AGM President, Robert Milton. The numbers suggested that over 90 airlines would still be unable to issue an electronic ticket by the deadline. And although we had managed to achieve over 2,600 IETs, around 32% of interline tickets would still be on paper.

There were two options. Either we took the hard line, which would not have been an issue at Board level but might have upset the rank and file, or we agreed to a limited extension. I had to reconcile my "No targets, no business" motto with IATA's role as an association that wanted all its members on board. Eventually, I suggested extending the deadline by another six months until May 2008. This was carefully thought out. By making sure the deadline was before the next AGM, when all major decisions such as this are debated by the airlines, there was no way IATA could extend it. I had made it absolutely clear that past May 2008, there would not be so much as an extra second, no matter what.

CS and Robert agreed to the proposal and we presented the plan to the Board. The discussion was passionate, but reasonable and constructive. The last to speak was the Saudi Arabian Airlines CEO, Khalid Abdullah Almolhem, who argued passionately for a short extension. In the end we were left with a two-pronged solution: apply the existing deadline to the airlines that could be ready for 100% ET by 31 December 2007 and grant a six-month extension to those few airlines that required it.

Even then, some carriers were not satisfied with this and asked for more time. They had correctly worked out that the Board would not be meeting again until after the new deadline and so there would be no further options to extend. This frightened them. I spent an hour chatting with Katsuo Haneda of JAL, trying to persuade him that the new deadline was realistic while he was warning that other airlines would support his call for a further extension. Other discussions went on all day, with a one-year postponement being pushed hard. Work was started on the text of a motion a few like-minded airlines were ready to submit to the AGM even if that meant having to go through a secret ballot vote. It was an exceptional situation but at the very least I was determined it would be handled properly.

We talked and talked. Groups broke off for separate discussions and then rejoined the main debate, a process that went on all night. There were some really odd conversations. For example, airlines from the same country were adopting radically different positions. All Nippon Airways was saying it could easily meet the deadline but Japan Airlines was adamant that the deadline be postponed by one year. Guess which airline fared better in the following couple of years?

And then, to top it all, I was served with an injunction from a Canadian court to stop the ET discussions because the authorities were concerned that we were raising antitrust issues. Obviously, we can't discuss ticket prices and the like at an AGM in case we get accused of price fixing. The court clearly thought we were treading a fine line but actually what an airline charged a passenger was completely irrelevant. I had no time for such distractions. I told my team to keep working at full speed and to ignore the injunction. I said we would worry about a court battle later, although to be honest I was convinced from the start that there was no basis to the injunction.

So on it went. CS Chew was woken up at 3am to smooth over some disagreement or other. I was lucky to have both him and Robert Milton on my side. They were both very open and honest and always available. Their determination helped me keep IATA from splitting in two and was absolutely necessary to the final result.

In the morning, Robert was able to bang the gavel on an agreement. End-May 2008 would bring to a close the reign of the paper ticket.

Celebration on the Bosphorus

On 1 June 2008, the aviation world was 100% ET. Out of 560 airlines worldwide only 34 did not make the deadline and they represented just 0.1% of BSP operations. That 34 included only four IATA members. The following day at the IATA AGM in Istanbul, thousands of shredded paper tickets descended like confetti on the participating CEOs in celebration of the success of the industry initiative. Aviation was the first industry to truly enter the paperless world.

We had reached a milestone in aviation and the travel experience of 2 billion-plus passengers would be a lot better for it. Eliminating paper has saved the industry $3 billion a year and the equivalent of 50,000 mature trees annually. In just four years, we had proven to the world that even though IATA was a small international organization, it was relevant to its members and could drive industry change on a massive scale. The dream had become a reality.

ET also laid the foundations for the success of the entire StB program, as the same principles were applied to other StB projects, from self-service check-in to e-freight. Today, a passenger can check in online or use a self-service kiosk at the airport. The boarding pass can be stored as a bar code on a mobile phone. And the journey can be tailor-made, perhaps booking lounge access with an economy fare or a certain type of meal. All of these projects had their own challenges and their own stories. But all of them followed the same pattern as ET and each was only made possible because of the groundwork laid by the founding StB project.

So long live ET. I sent every airline a framed copy of a paper ticket as a reminder that our hard work and cooperation ended in success. If you still have a paper ticket, send it to your local museum. That's where it belongs.

Good and bad technology

Aviation and technology are inseparable. You can't put 100 metric tons of machine 40,000 feet into the air—safely—without a lot of technical know-how. The problem is that this relationship has clouded judgment, and IT is often seen as just that—IT. CEOs need to remember that we are really talking about a commercial and marketing tool.

Distribution highlights the issue. In the old days, when global distribution systems were dominant, the likes of Amadeus and Gallileo were run by IT guys. And airline CEOs listened to what they were saying because they had no idea of the technology behind the systems. This meant airline CEOs didn't have a true understanding of the value of these systems. And remember, this was originally an airline idea, one they couldn't develop because of lack of funds.

It was Bob Crandall, the legendary CEO of American Airlines, who first really understood how to leverage IT as a commercial distribution tool. I remembered what Bob had done and also drew on my experience with Galileo and OPODO. When I joined IATA I wanted to bring distribution back under airline control, and so, set up a project to see if we could build and run a global distribution system. I asked Rakesh Gangwal, former CEO of US Airways, to spearhead the project. Unfortunately, this opportunity for change was never grasped mainly because airline lawyers were very nervous about airlines getting involved with each other. Rakesh went on to become Worldspan CEO and a major influence in one of the most successful Indian carriers, Indigo. And I still think a new distribution system was a good idea and that GDSs have taken too much money from airlines for too long. It led to me calling the GDSs "leeches" at the 2010 AGM and causing a real storm. But the tactic worked. IATA has now launched a "New Distribution Capability" project and the GDSs look like being willing participants.

Social media is another new "technology" and again I think CEOs are in danger of missing the point. I see social media mainly as a distribution tool. It is not just about information or marketing but rather needs to be integrated with those sides of the business to advance distribution techniques. When you see a company like Google get involved, buying ITA, a major supplier of airline software, you have to worry that an airline ticket will become a commodity. This would be a major problem for the airlines.

With any change, airlines will face the usual dilemma. To innovate and be first to market or wait for the teething troubles to be ironed out and follow fast behind. As Alitalia CEO, I was definitely a fast follower. It was a sensible strategy. Being an innovator is a risky and expensive business. And while the idea for change may be good, it's unlikely to be a perfect fit for the market at the beginning. It will take a few months worth of tweaks to get the product or system right. And that is where being a fast follower comes in.

At Alitalia, I took a new cargo IT program, not long after launch, called "Fast" that was quickly acquired by all the major cargo airlines. We were able to refine the product even further and we had stolen a march on most of our competitors. The program made Alitalia a lot of money. Years later, during a visit to Japan as IATA DG, Nippon Cargo CEO Masayo Yamaguchi told me that they were still using the program. They were more impressed with the fact that I was the person who had made the Cargo IT program into such a practical product than that I was the IATA DG.

There are always a lot of good ideas out there. Creativity isn't the problem. Look at the leadership role in the industry being played by my good friend Louis Chênevert, CEO of United Technologies Corporation, for example. He is constantly redrawing the boundaries of what is possible. The obstacle to progress is the need for deep pockets. Look at the aircraft manufacturers. Putting a completely new aircraft into production is a multi-billion dollar gamble. It's why you don't see new aircraft every other year and why there are so few manufacturers. Of course, we need new aircraft from time to time, just as we need new technology and software. So there has to be something in it for the innovator. As long as there is a constant push for the product to be improved, once a company gets ahead, it can stay ahead. A company must challenge itself to stay the best.

Ahmed Shafik, Prime Minister of Egypt

Pope John Paul II

Neil Armstrong, astronaut and the first person to walk on the Moon

Ban Ki-moon, Secretary General of the United Nations

Lee Kuan Yew, first Prime Minister of the Republic of Singapore

Janet Napolitano, United States Secretary of Homeland Security

Dato' Sri Mohd Najib Bin Tun Haji Abdul Razak, Prime Minister of Malaysia

HM King Abdullah II of Jordan

Muammar al-Gaddafi, Prime Minister of Libya

Muhammad Naji al-Otari, Prime Minister of Syria (right)

Mwai Kibaki, President of Kenya

Sebastián Piñera, President of Chile

Kang Ki Sop, President of the General Administration of Civil Aviation, North Korea

Igor Levitin, Minister of Transport, Russia

H.E. Professor Dr Boediono, Vice President of the Republic of Indonesia

Ricardo Martinelli, President of Panama

CHAPTER SIX

The Future is Green

Environmental initiatives, including airspace issues and the EU ETS

The case for the defence

Let me be clear. I am not a climate change expert. But for me the evidence plainly shows that aviation is not a major offender when it comes to the environment. In fact, it is by far the most proactive industry in the world in terms of environmental mitigation. And it could do even better if governments and big oil companies actually lived up to their green claims and supported the industry's efforts rather than hinder them.

The environmental problem has always been there. The US Environmental Protection Agency first issued proposals about aircraft emissions in the early 1970s. It has really gathered pace in the last decade though, as climate change became a media headline around the world. It is a legitimate concern but many green organizations have manipulated the facts. Aviation has been an easy target. For environmentalists, airlines became the worst polluter, the antithesis of the green brigade that "cared" about the planet. Who isn't aware of a big jet flying overhead? This simple emotive image has proved a useful tool for activists more interested in capturing votes or new members than in effective measures that would make our planet greener.

A few more facts should set the record straight. Modern aircraft are more fuel efficient than a compact car. A jet coming off the production line today is nearly 80% more fuel efficient per passenger seat kilometre than one delivered in the 1960s. And with a load factor historically averaging 76%, aircraft have far greater occupancy levels than other forms of transport. Moreover, the vast majority of aircraft emissions (around 80%) come from flights over 1,500km for which there is no practical alternative. The list could go on and on.

There is hard evidence that aviation takes the environment seriously too. Look at how the industry dealt with noise. For a long time, this was the biggest complaint against airlines. In the 1970s, the fast development of airports and residential building close to airports had an impact on local communities living in the airport neighbourhood. A lot of good work was done by airports but the real issue was producing comparable or even more power from jet engines while reducing noise.

Government regulations emerged in the 1980s. The European Commission proposed tough noise standards. A lot of aircraft wouldn't have taken to the sky if these new laws were ruthlessly applied. There was a so-called "Hush Kit" battle (named after the hardware applied to engines to make them quieter) between European and US regulators, which was won by the United States. I was involved in these discussions because I was a member of the Advisory Board of Pratt and Whitney and the European Commission President was my former boss, Romano Prodi. The EC regulation was tough but so was the US reaction. If the legislation had passed it would have meant that a significant number of aircraft operated by the US airlines would have been banned from flying to Europe. ICAO had the mandate to handle airspace issues, and while it deemed the EC initiative illegal, it did set noise standards that all airlines had to meet. These became more stringent over time, so airlines had no choice but to ensure their aircraft became quieter. Today, the latest generation of high bypass ratio engines means aircraft are 50% quieter than they were just ten years ago.

Examples such as this show how green organizations have often distorted the truth. And they weren't the only ones to lose touch with reality. Respected personalities, such as the Archbishop of London, Richard Chartres, also entered the debate. Referring to CO_2 emissions, he actually proclaimed that "flying abroad for a foreign holiday is a sin against the planet". Not the most well thought out sermon.

Still, statements such as this egged on the other green associations and campaigners. They understood that they could benefit from this debate. Raising money and receiving subsidies becomes much more likely when the debate becomes heated and fought in the public domain.

From the beginning of my time at IATA, the Corporate Communications Department was receiving requests regarding IATA's position on the environment. I must admit we had no clear policy. With no future plans or any defined strategy, we had to limit our answers to a blunt, single fact: aviation is responsible for 1.8% of man-made carbon emissions. The figure came from the United Nations and it could be easily and advantageously compared with the 18% of the car transportation output or the 35% emitted by electricity and manufacturing plants. We argued this clearly demonstrated the small role of aviation in the CO_2 emissions hit parade. It was all true but it was no excuse for the lack of an environmental strategy.

Despite the magic 1.8% number, the pressure on aviation was growing. Green campaigns were building momentum. They pointed at contrails in the sky as an obvious sign of airline emissions. They asked how a massive four-engined jet flying from one end of the world to the other could be doing anything other than harm.

The misinformation had to stop. I decided it was time to fight back in a more coherent and structured fashion.

Widening the focus

I took over IATA in the aftermath of 9/11. The industry had different priorities then and the environmental debate was lost in the struggle to survive. One crisis after another battered our member airlines. On the question of the environment, we simply hid behind the 1.8% figure and got on with other business. But it became increasingly clear as time went on that this lack of a strategy would no longer suffice. I had some initial conversations with a few of our Board members but the subject held little interest for most of them. The first time the Board formally discussed the environmental issue was in December 2003, but this was mainly because the industry had to present its position at the 2004 ICAO Assembly, which had the environment on its agenda. The industry position was not very strong. We said we were concerned by unilateral European environmental taxes and emphasized the need for ICAO to remain vigilant. It was logical to conclude that paying a tax in one country did nothing for global climate change. It just put fares up a bit and the money went straight into the government bank account, doing nothing for the environment. Our basic gameplan remained unchanged: prepare data on aviation's contribution to global emissions, comparing it with other modes of transportation.

At the February 2004 Assembly, ICAO approved a resolution urging states to refrain from the unilateral imposition of taxes until the next ICAO Assembly in 2007. It didn't excite me much at first but I came to see this as quite an important result. Stopping the introduction of carbon taxes gave me a three-year window to build consensus on a strategy that could be presented at the next ICAO Assembly. I had already become convinced that whatever the strategy was going to be, it had to generate excitement beyond the industry. I didn't want governments picking on aviation, saying this is what the public wants.

In 2004 though, it is probably true to say that some of our customers were uncomfortable with the idea of flying because of the climate change debate. The green campaign was ramping up and aviation was firmly fixed in its sights as the chief villain. We were not in the wrong but nobody believed us. We could no longer muddle our way through. The environmental issue had to be met head-on.

The first challenge was to understand what airlines thought about the aviation environmental problem and, just as importantly, what governments thought about it. It was necessary to understand not only what we should do but also to put any proposals in a regulatory context. My efforts got off to a bad start. I went to the United States, where my meetings included a visit to the Air Transport Association of America (ATA). Try as I might I couldn't sell the idea of an environmental strategy. In essence, I was told the United States had not signed the Kyoto Protocol, and therefore the environmental problem didn't concern them. And the Bush Administration was right behind this position.

Shortly afterwards I met with Minister Yang Yuanyuan of the Chinese Civil Aviation (CAAC). I knew him well as we had met at a conference in Singapore a year earlier. I had made the keynote speech and ended by saying that aviation was global and that we all communicated in English, the *lingua franca* of the industry. As I knew the Minister was there, I highlighted the fact that the Chinese were going it alone by having their air traffic controllers communicate in Chinese with Chinese carriers. I said this was a safety risk because Western pilots in the same airspace cannot understand what is going on. The audience was shocked but not the Minister. He spoke after me and expertly put the ball back in my court, saying he was sure that IATA would help train the 5,000 or so controllers in very quick time. We talked afterwards and together with Berlitz, set up a very successful technical language school. It paved the way for greater cooperation with the Chinese and we have seen some spectacular results, especially in safety.

In fact, in 2005, safety was the number one priority for China rather than the environment. Minister Yang appreciated IATA's role in assisting CAAC but the environment was simply not part of the package. Having drawn a blank with the United States and China, a couple of months later I went to New Delhi to meet the Indian Minister of Aviation, Praful Patel. Minister Patel was a visionary man who understood aviation's importance to a country of over 1 billion people. But the answer here was similar to the one I received in China. The priority was putting aviation back on track after years of inaction. In Africa, I also hit a brick wall. Their biggest issue was safety. The continent had a hull loss rate that had been embarrassingly high for many years—over ten times higher than the world average in fact.

It would be fair to say the outcome of my world tour was not very encouraging.

Getting prepared

I had stalled on the global stage but in Europe the climate change debate was moving up through the gears. It wasn't long before the European Parliament initiated a study on the environmental impact of aviation. Around this time, in the United Kingdom, the greens organized noisy demonstrations, with crowds of people camping in the Heathrow area while the third runway was under discussion in the UK Parliament.

The media kept on asking the same question: "What is the industry position?" The magic 1.8% number was not enough to feed the growing frenzy. Aviation was losing the battle.

Despite the poor answers from various corners of the globe to my environmental questioning, I was determined to convince the Board that a wait-and-see strategy was not an option. As far as I was concerned, IATA had to define a position for discussion at the Board meeting in Tokyo in December 2005. Airline CEOs listened politely but had different opinions, with some wanting us to emphasize the 20% fuel efficiency we had achieved over the last decade while others took a more aggressive stance, weighing the 1.8% contribution of aviation to carbon emissions against its 8% contribution to global GDP. Nevertheless, the discussions were very positive and in December 2005 the Board endorsed what we came to refer to as the Four Pillar Strategy: new technology, more effective operations, more efficient infrastructure and positive economic measures.

Technology is an important driver for progress. Environmentally, it has helped with the accelerated development of alternative fuels as well as with more advanced materials and systems for airframes and engines. Avionics for enhanced air traffic management systems also come under this heading. More effective operations covered fleet renewal, increasing load factors and a multitude of details such as electric towing vehicles and using airport power rather than having aircraft run their auxiliary power units. More efficient infrastructure can make a real difference. By addressing airspace and airport inefficiency, governments and infrastructure providers have the potential to eliminate up to 12% of aviation's CO_2 emissions. The implementation of a Single European Sky and the US NextGen air transport system are a top priority. Last, but not least, economic measures should be used to boost the research and the development of new technologies rather than act as a tool to limit demand. Punitive taxes do not improve environmental performance. An emission trading scheme could be a cost-efficient solution, but the system has to be implemented on a global basis under the leadership of ICAO.

For once, I had an easy time building consensus among the aviation partners. People were a bit surprised at the time, given the stormy relationships that existed between certain partners, but we all have the same commitment to enhanced performance and environmental mitigation. There was little in the way of competitive or business issues to cloud the talks. And the Four Pillar Strategy was a good one, spreading accountability so no one sector felt isolated. I took personal responsibility for having all our partners on board. Tom Enders of Airbus, Alan Mulally at Boeing, Eric Bachelet at CFM, Sir John Rose of Rolls Royce, Marion Blakey, former FAA Administrator and now Chairman of AIA, were among those with whom I talked. Northern European airlines such as SAS and Finnair were just as happy as their Southern counterparts with this unity. They felt the industry finally had a proactive approach. Lufthansa was also pleased, particularly with the technical aspect. Asian and US leaders, such as Gerard Arpey at American and Fred Smith at FedEx, also appreciated that this was a balanced solution that gave the industry time to adapt while sending a strong message. Aviation was the first sector to meet this challenge head on.

The biggest surprise for me was dealing with airports and ANSPs. For the first time, we were quick to agree with Alexander Ter Kuile, Head of the Civil

Air Navigation Services Organization (CANSO), and Robert Aaronson, the ACI Chief. This strong camaraderie meant a lot to me and the entire value chain being on the same wavelength on how to approach the environment issue had to be made known to the general public. I didn't want the strategy presented with an IATA flag even though we were responsible for mobilizing the industry. Everybody needed to be involved from first to last if this was to work, each partner responsible for a piece of the jigsaw.

Apart from the Four Pillar Strategy, we identified five key points that had to be stressed every time the environment was on the agenda:

- *International aviation was excluded from Kyoto because ICAO was the most appropriate United Nations agency to find and implement a solution.*
- *Air transport is not a major source of greenhouse gas emissions as it contributes just 1.8% of CO_2 of man-made emissions.*
- *Air transport is not the most polluting form of transportation and fuel efficiency had improved 20% over the last decade.*
- *Aviation is not paying tax on fuel as it pays $42 billion annually for its own infrastructure.*
- *Air transport makes the global village a reality.*

The industry under pressure

While all this was going on, the 2006 Stern Report on the economics of climate change was published and the evidence gathered led to a simple conclusion: the benefit of strong and early action far outweighed the economic cost of that action.

The fact that had the biggest impact from the public perspective was an acknowledgment that aviation was a fast growing business. The report predicted we would increase our share of man-made emissions to 5% by 2050. This was the point at which the Archbishop of London piped up and declared flying a sin, in effect giving the newspaper headline writers a day off because that sort of story just writes itself.

So while we had a much improved environmental strategy, we were still some way off winning the public relations battle. I pushed aviation's credentials every chance I got and we were certainly winning respect for our work. But for many, that big jet in the sky had to be trouble for the environment. They couldn't see past that image of a roaring jet engine and contrails overhead—which the environmentalists exploited to the full.

By the start of 2007, I knew it was time for another leap forward. The months ahead were going to be busy ones for the environmental agenda and we had to have a response ready. The main reason for the increased activity was the Intergovernmental Panel on Climate Change (IPCC) Fourth Assessment Report on Climate Change in May 2007. The IPCC Chairman was Dr Rajendra Pachauri and the report upped aviation's CO_2 contribution to 2% of man-made emissions. Pachauri is a serious scientist with great personal charisma. He has the patience to listen to others and is always ready to provide reasonable and achievable counsel. After a few meetings in Geneva and New Delhi, I built up a personal relationship with him and he was among the first to hear about our Four Pillar environment strategy. His suggestions did a lot for our credibility and future success.

Under Pachauri's guidance, the IPCC shared the 2007 Nobel Peace Prize with Al Gore. I got to meet the former US Vice President at the house of a very influential friend of mine in Geneva, Thierry Lombard of the Lombard Odier private banking. Lombard Odier has a history dating back to the 18th century and is mentioned in Jules Verne's famous novel, *Le Voyage dans La Lune*, when the bank is requested to fund the expedition. Dinners at Thierry's house are always very special. His house captures the essence of Switzerland with a wonderful countryside setting and a sophisticated interior décor. This sophistication was reflected in the menus and the erudition of the host. You need to do your homework though—conversations could flow from international affairs to the stock market, and even the value of sponsorship (Thierry sponsors the Hydroptère, the fastest hydrofoil on the sea). I remember an anecdote from our first invitation to the house, just a couple of blocks away from our own home, that neatly captures the spirit of Thierry's world. My wife, Elena, asked him how long the house had been in the family. It was a polite question to which the answer usually varies from a few years to a few decades. Thierry answered with a shrug: "Several hundred years."

The dinner with Al Gore was a great one. If Dr Pachauri is the scientist, Al Gore is the inspired politician who understands the public impact of the climate change challenge and puts his strong spokesman skills at the service of a world campaign. I outlined IATA's vision to the former US Vice President and he was very impressed. His questions were incisive and very different to the usual response of politicians, which is based on why something can't be done. His vision was countered by Thierry's pragmatic banker skills and I learned a lot about what would be strong yet achievable targets.

All things considered, the IPCC 2% figure was a good one for aviation. Yes, it had increased slightly from our magic 1.8% number, but this was coming from a respected UN agency and so couldn't be disputed by the greens. Try as they might, they couldn't make 2% sound like it was a lot. Aviation was a relatively minor offender according to the statistics. Having the moral high ground was just the start, however. I wanted to hammer home this advantage and dispel the myth that airlines are an environmental disaster once and for all. We had to make the public understand aviation was serious about its environmental responsibilities.

It was another gamble. If I set a challenging target for reducing emissions, what would happen if that target slipped by? IATA and the airlines would lose their credibility and aviation might never recover the lost ground. Environmental taxes and curtailed operations would be just a few of the penalties on offer for our failure.

I had set up a small IATA team, led by Philippe Rochat, former Secretary General of ICAO, who was IATA's Environment Director. We discussed what we should do next. I also referred to the conversations I had with the two Nobel Peace Prize winners, Rajendra Pachauri and Al Gore, as to what an environmental roadmap should look like. However, we kept our work confidential and no word leaked out beyond IATA. The only information that we chose to disclose was the fuel efficiency results and this was because they had been partly brought about by earlier campaigns and so couldn't be ignored.

The 2007 AGM in June in Vancouver was fast approaching. Although there was a huge debate going on about electronic ticketing, I knew I had to say something strong about the environment. I started asking our members if we should step up the pace on the environment but most felt we should take things slowly and that the small CO_2 savings we were making would buy us some time. To be honest, many airline CEOs were more taken with the idea of fuel efficiency saving money rather than CO_2 emissions. There was nothing wrong with that. Even though their focus was on reducing fuel to save money, the environment still benefited. In any case, most of these airlines weren't facing the same intensity of environmental pressure as Northern European airlines. I warned them, though, that this would change in time. Better to get behind an industry position now than leave themselves open to complaint in the future. I lost count of the number of times someone said to me: "Giovanni, our contribution is only 2% and we have a good track record." True, but my problem was that very few people outside the industry had any knowledge of all the work that had been undertaken.

The idea of a tough target was a very similar problem to the one I faced with the e-ticketing initiative. Every airline was different and so had different ideas about what could, and should, be achieved. In the United States, there was no sense of urgency, the US Government not having signed the Kyoto Protocol. In Asia and the Middle East, the priority was getting ready to conquer new markets with the rapid growth of their fleets backed by large government investment. Africa's environmental culture was virtually non-existent and desperately lacking resources. Even Europe was not as united as I had hoped. The United Kingdom and Northern Europe—particularly Mats Jansson at SAS—were eager to push the bar as high as possible, to respond to the green parties that were gaining momentum in the political arena. Southern Europeans were not so motivated, concerned more with costs and under-performing national economies.

It left me with a difficult decision. It always is difficult when you have to set a target, but the airlines were nervous because they now understood that IATA was being run as a business and it expected targets to be met. As I have mentioned, I had taken the IATA job to implement change. And I reasoned that individual airlines were understandably engaged in the tough business of making money, leaving them little time to make sensible, long-term judgments on the environmental issue. IATA's role was "to represent, lead and serve the airline industry". I turned again to the notion of leadership. It would have been easy to delay the announcement, to find a consensus, and it is usually the sensible decision because it limits risk.

Building a consensus would have taken too much time, however. I knew going out alone—setting a target without consultation—was a risk. But risk, properly managed, is a key component of the CEO job. To lead, you have to love challenges and you have to love risk.

"I have a dream..."

I decided I would present the industry strategy and targets directly to the Vancouver AGM, in front of a group of 600 industry stakeholders and more than 300 journalists representing various media worldwide. I was going to do this without a proper assessment by the Board. In effect, I would ask the AGM to endorse my State of the Industry report, which would include the environmental targets. This was a calculated risk because I knew going through the proper channels at the Board would at the very least slow down the process and perhaps force the abandonment of my target altogether.

I didn't have any figures in mind, more a goal we could aspire to. In this instance, I felt any mention of specific numbers would crystallize opposition faster than it would unite the industry. And I felt talking in terms of a dream might prove more inspirational. It worked very well for JFK when he announced he wanted to put a man on the moon before the end of the decade, even though NASA at the time had no idea how to do that. But his speech allowed the United States to recover lost ground and ultimately win the space race. Neil Armstrong realized Kennedy's dream and in 2010 IATA gave him its Global Aviation Leadership Award (GALA). Neil is no longer with us, his passing, like his life, free from any special public ceremony. He was such a down-to-Earth man considering his status as the first human to set foot on another world. But never doubt his courage, determination and leadership.

His remarkable acceptance speech for the GALA honour actually mirrored my aspirations in 2007. He recounted man's attempts to circumnavigate the Earth, noting how the time to do so has come down from three years to just over 90 minutes. Toward the end of his speech he said: "I have had the privilege of working for and working with remarkably skilled people." This was typical Neil.

Prior to the Vancouver AGM, I needed to capture that same kind of raw appeal to colleagues to work with me to make the world a better place. I had to appeal to the heart of the industry, not the brains of the CEOs. I called for a meeting of my IATA environmental team. We discussed what I would say at the AGM in June. Every sentence and slide was analyzed in great detail and by the end of May we had a final text. I had to touch the audience, providing not only a vision of the future but a strong foundation from which we could reach out.

As I went up to the podium, I knew that I would be putting my personal reputation on the line. If I got this wrong, airlines would become a laughing stock for the green organizations. I had only informed the Board Chairman, CS Chew of Singapore Airlines, that I would deliver a strong, forward-looking speech, but as is the tradition at IATA, I didn't disclose anything else.

The next 40 minutes were indeed some of the most intense of my life. When delivering a big speech, I usually concentrate on a couple of people sitting in the front row. I follow their expression to get a feeling of how the message is being perceived. On this occasion two Board members were the focus of my attention, Wolfgang Mayrhuber, CEO of Lufthansa, and Jean-Cyril Spinetta, the Chairman and CEO of Air France. I started my speech with an update on the economics of the industry. We were chronically in the red as usual, and I used the environment to counteract this. Here, I stated, "Our track record is good, reducing noise by 75% and improving fuel efficiency 70%. The billions invested in new aircraft will make airlines 25% more fuel-efficient by 2010…but we have been silent in our success and we have now a reputation crisis." I explained our Four Pillar Strategy as part of the solution. I said the commitment of IATA, of our members, and of our partners was encouraging. Against this background, I further explained we had to find the courage and strength to fly higher. No other industry had the same level of sophisticated technology, was able to work in the most difficult conditions at 30,000 feet at 30 degrees centigrade below zero. "I don't have all the answers but our industry started with a vision that we could fly," I continued calmly. "The Wright Brothers turned that dream into a reality and look at where we are now. We can see the potential building blocks for a carbon-free future."

That last sentence created an electric atmosphere. There was an audible buzz. When I mentioned carbon-free future, I looked at Wolfgang. I'm not sure if he was looking at me because his eyes were wide in astonishment. It was Wolfgang the engineer who couldn't support the idea that a carbon-free future is possible, considering the current state of technology. I was careful to note that the concept was an aspiration; and to achieve the vision we had to set targets and a roadmap that would be my responsibility to bring to the next Board meeting for review. Wolfgang and Jean-Cyril relaxed a little at this and at the end a long applause concluded the presentation.

Environmentally-speaking, a lot had happened in my 40 minutes on the podium. From being in a defensive position the industry had suddenly propelled itself forward and made the most committed approach to the environment of any industry. We would have a carbon-free future. And on our way to that future we would obviously hit the milestone of being carbon-neutral. In effect, we could fly more—grow our businesses— while keeping our level of CO_2 emissions constant. I knew the bigger battle of concrete targets still lay ahead but my speech received a huge round of applause. The media loved the story too. The courage of our industry was clear to see and the public perception of aviation started to improve. All we had to do now was fix a deadline and find the money and technology to make the vision possible!

A united approach

June 2007 was also notable for a significant strengthening of the IATA environmental team.

We met with the World Wildlife Fund (WWF), known worldwide for its dedication to the environmental cause. WWF is a large organization with offices all around the world and with a total staff of over 7,000 people. Tom Windmuller and I met with John Leape and Paul Steele. The discussion was productive and the WWF was quite impressed with the airlines' achievements and commitment. They didn't realize IATA was quite so active on behalf of its members or that we could set the standards that determine the travel experience. We ended the meeting and left our experts to discuss the way forward for an effective partnership between the two organizations. The following week, Tom came to see me and said that Paul Steele could very well be interested in coming to work for IATA. I had been impressed by Paul's leadership and was surprised to hear of his interest in joining IATA. Being responsible for an entire workforce, was he really ready to run a small team with a handful of industry experts? Although the team was short on quantity, it was high on quality. And we had taken full page advertisements in *The Economist* so weren't being shy. A couple of weeks later, I met with Paul and finalized the agreement to have him join us. I was very pleased for two reasons. One, we had the right person on board, which was very reassuring for the future of our strategy. Two, the hard work that IATA had done so far was starting to pay off. The external perception of the association was clearly changing, to the extent that someone of Paul's calibre would think of working for IATA. I asked Paul why he wanted to join IATA. He said he appreciated my passion and that the challenge of influencing an environmental strategy for one of the top global industry sectors was just too good to ignore.

Post-AGM 2007, our environmental work changed speed and its *modus operandi*. Once again, I turned toward the idea of targets, a demonstrable show of commitment. IATA's Safety, Operations and Infrastructure (SO&I) division, under the leadership of Günther Matschnigg, former COO at Austrian Airlines, pushed hard in finding new efficiencies and new ways of working. Together with the forecasts provided by IATA's talented Chief Economist, Brian Pearce, this helped formulate the roadmap. The task was nothing less than to identify how and when we could become a carbon-free industry. As part of that goal, the environment team was told to finalize a date for when we achieve carbon-neutral growth (CNG). This would be a tough enough target in itself. We had to stabilize our emissions output even if traffic increased as expected at around 5% per year. This was an important objective because it would kill the story that aviation's CO_2 emissions would grow. The 2007 IPCC Report said we would be 3% of man-made emissions by 2050, an improvement on the 5% cited by the Stern Report but still an increase. I wanted to nip that argument in the bud. We would be carbon-neutral in the short term and carbon-free in the longer term.

Our first priority was to build a model that would allow aviation to maintain its contribution to global carbon emissions at 2% despite forecast growth. We asked McKinsey to work with us and the model suggested that 2% was doable, as long as the whole value chain committed to achieve the necessary efficiency gains. The model took into account that airlines would modernize their fleet, technology development was expected from the manufacturers, and governments would have to commit to ATM investments and finally implement the Single European Sky and NextGen. The study also acknowledged that IATA member airlines were planning test flights with biofuels and this would be an important development going forward.

The work IATA was doing was having a big impact. ICAO couldn't ignore what was going on and Roberto Kobeh Gonzalez, Dr Assad Kotaite's successor, drove the 36th ICAO Assembly towards a position similar to that of the industry. That was a difficult thing to achieve. IATA had trouble finding consensus among its member airlines. I can only imagine what it takes to bring 193 countries to agreement. The BRIC countries (Brazil, Russia, India and China) are a particular issue in environmental terms. The problem is ICAO and the UNFCCC have different operating rules. In a nutshell, the Chicago Convention doesn't discriminate—all states are treated the same. This isn't the situation with UNFCCC guidelines and many countries don't want to lose the advantages of being a "developing" nation.

But Kobeh and his very effective Secretary General, Raymond Benjamin, found a solution with a great deal of patience and intelligent team work. Their internal restructuring of ICAO also helped. I have enjoyed a special relationship with all the ICAO leaders, Assad Kotaite, Roberto Kobeh and Raymond Benjamin. It helped that ICAO and IATA had similar histories, inaugurated in 1945 with the aim of supporting civil aviation. We both wanted the industry to be safer, more efficient and more environmentally-friendly. It's even harder for ICAO than IATA of course, as it is confined by UN procedures. Also a lot of governments were now sending environmental specialists to ICAO meetings, stifling the process with detail.

In spring 2008, IATA held an Aviation and Environment Summit in Geneva. Speakers included Scott Carson at Boeing, who had taken on the tough job of following Alan Mulally. Alan had left a real mark in the industry and left to run Ford, where he has made a huge difference. He is still considered to be on the aviation gang. But Scott did a great job too. I flew to Seattle to meet Scott just a week after he had taken office and he embraced the environmental mission straight away. Tom Enders of Airbus has been equally strong in supporting our green strategy. At the Summit, Scott, Tom and 11 other major companies and organizations pledged to work for a carbon-free future. The "Aviation Industry Commitment to Action on Climate Change" declaration demonstrated the united industry approach and was a clear statement of intent. Without a common strategy and a precise commitment to reduce our environmental impact, our future would have been at risk.

The road to Copenhagen, Part 1

IATA was invited to present its story at a preparatory meeting to the 15th Conference of Parties (COP15), the foremost summit on climate change. The preparatory meeting was held in May 2009 in Copenhagen in anticipation of the main event in December of that year. The invitation was a surprise as it was the first time the association had been asked to participate in a relevant environment event not as a defendant but as an industry leading by example. It was a great boost to the work we were doing.

The Copenhagen meeting gathered thousands of participants as well as the global media. The United Nations Secretary General Ban Ki-moon opened the event with a constructive presentation, followed by Al Gore who delivered a vibrant and passionate speech. The next speaker was Dr Pachauri who had been kept abreast of all the latest aviation initiatives. I was then called to the podium to present IATA's story and aviation's commitment to environmental mitigation. I was the only representative of an industry sector to be invited to speak. In my presentation I emphasized the work that thousands of people had done on behalf of aviation and the environment. It was a great success. Many of the green agencies that had previously identified aviation as the enemy of climate change came to congratulate me. Moreover, during the evening function at a wonderful old palace in the center of the city, Secretary General Ban Ki-moon invited me to visit him at the UN New York headquarters to update him on the industry's achievements.

By the time of the IATA AGM in Kuala Lumpur in June 2009 we had come far enough to take the next step. The timeframe for our targets had to be announced. Otherwise, we would be in danger of losing momentum. We had managed to slow the external pressure on the industry's environmental record, but it hadn't stopped, and there were signs that it could increase again. Some wanted aviation included in climate change agreements. These were formulated at the national level, though, and so were entirely inappropriate for an industry that operated across national boundaries.

Another group of experts were supporting the so-called Maldives Adaptation Levy, a proposal for a $6-tax per airline ticket that would generate $10 billion. This money would fill the coffers of the Kyoto Protocol's Adaptation Fund to help finance climate adaptation projects in developing countries. Other tax proposals had a similar strategy. Repeatedly I explained how strange it was that an industry that was in deep financial trouble and had the slimmest of profit margins—if any at all—was still considered a source of revenue and the sole target of environmental taxes. On top of that, we had already presented a daring environmental strategy. We had promised to do more than any other industry sector.

A few weeks before the AGM, I went to Delhi to update Dr Pachauri on the recent developments in our carbon-free initiative. While there, I also met with Indian Transport Minister Patel and the recently appointed Indian Minister for Environment, Jairam Ramesh. Ramesh received me wearing the typical Indian kurta, but his opening gambit was anything but traditional. With a big smile on his face, he said: "I am pleased to meet the $10-billion man who will solve many of our environmental problems." I was surprised by this unusual greeting and probably the expression on my face gave away my amazement. The Minister immediately clarified. "A meeting of environment ministers and the European Commission is currently taking place in New Delhi. The idea of a levy on passenger tickets could help a lot. And its implementation is very simple. We are simply asking IATA to add the appropriate box to a ticket, cash the amount levied and credit it to the Kyoto Adaptation Fund."

I explained why this was not acceptable under any circumstances. Aviation, at just 2% of man-made CO_2 emissions, was going to foot the bill for an entire climate change program. Moreover, IATA couldn't raise monies for a fund that was lacking in details. The meeting was pleasant enough but I cut it short. As soon as I jumped in the car, I started fighting this crazy idea, making a number of phone calls to alert the industry of the danger coming up.

There was an upside though. I realized the emergence of these new tax ideas could be used as leverage to get the industry's agreement on target dates for our environmental strategy at the forthcoming AGM. I needed all the help I could get. Word was out that I was pushing for target dates and just as with e-ticketing, the excuses were coming in thick and fast. The Air Transport Association (ATA) of America sent me a letter saying they could not "support having a carbon-neutral growth (CNG) commitment any time before 2020". As soon as I arrived in KL, smaller airlines raised similar objections. The global financial crisis, which was now biting deep, had forced them to abandon fleet renewal plans. So meeting tough environmental targets would be impossible for them, they said. I explained to them all that the postponement of our goal would weaken our position considerably and that the forthcoming Copenhagen Conference (COP15) could well see a push for the Maldives Adaptation Levy or a similar initiative. I promised these airlines that they would receive technical support from IATA regarding new routes and our environmental Go Teams would visit them to provide assistance regarding their fuel efficiency.

As I always say, no target, no business. I couldn't be swayed from a long-term goal by temporary problems. At the same time, I knew that achieving consensus among so many different airlines with so many different objectives and such different financial resources would be a very tough job indeed.

The Board of Governors Meeting was held the day before the start of the AGM as usual. Another letter from ATA arrived, this one more difficult to ignore as it contained some strong political warnings and was signed by all the US IATA member airlines. They were particularly worried that the target for carbon-neutral growth would boil down to carrier-specific dates. So, airline A would be tasked with becoming carbon-neutral by such-and-such a date. I called up some of the signatories to the letter and explained that not only the target but also the idea of individual commitment versus a collective goal had yet to be agreed. Rumours about the US carriers not supporting us were beginning to circulate, but I made sure I kept open the lines of communication. When issues like this arise, you need to be available personally. A formal written response would not be worth the paper it was written on. I needed to speak with the people involved and so I patiently waited for the arrival of the two US Board members, Gerard Arpey of American Airlines and David Bronczek of FedEx. It was a frank exchange, mainly centred on a North European–United States divide, but we set a window for the CNG target date and also agreed that it had to be an industry goal and not carrier specific. After further discussions centred on the needs of airlines in developing countries, we set the date for CNG: 2020. Finally we had backed up our Vancouver commitment to carbon-neutral growth with a real target for implementation. Coupled with the rest of our work on the roadmap, we now had three sequential goals: (1) a 1.5% average annual improvement in fuel efficiency from 2009 to 2020; (2) carbon-neutral growth from 2020; and (3) a 50% absolute reduction in carbon emissions by 2050 compared with 2005.

G8 connections

The Kuala Lumpur AGM was a great success and we again captured media headlines around the world. Many questioned our target, however. Was it Mission Impossible? Despite everything we had done, the idea that aviation simply be included in a follow-up to Kyoto was still floating around government circles.

I targeted the G8 meeting in L'Aquila in Italy in July 2009 for a response. The environment was a particularly crucial issue as L'Aquila, a wonderful medieval city, had been hit by a devastating earthquake just a couple of months before. Prior to the G8 meeting, I flew to Italy to discuss the issue with the Italian Prime Minister, Silvio Berlusconi. He was very positive and understood aviation's position. He went so far as to congratulate us for our efforts. But we had to have consensus from the G8 heads of state. And that meant I had to react quickly to gain consensus among their advisors.

I immediately called all the Board members of the G8 countries involved. They all reacted quickly, but the fastest ones were Wolfgang Mayrhuber of Lufthansa, Robert Milton of Air Canada, Haruka Nishimatsu of Japan Airlines and Dave Bronzcek of FedEx. To be honest, the United States was an easy sell because our strategy was now perfectly aligned with the US position. Dave had a good relationship with Carol Browner, the Head of the White House Office of Energy and Climate Change Policy. We went to visit her in her oak-panelled office in the White House and were impressed by her pro-industry approach. Ambassador Massolo also played an important role as Secretary General of the Italian Foreign Affairs Ministry. He chaired various meetings of the Sherpa Groups (advisors to the heads of state) that won the consensus we required. The G8 Meeting concluded that ICAO had sole jurisdiction over aviation environment matters. ICAO alone could decide what to do. It was a clear victory for the industry.

All of this happened within four days. It just goes to show the power of the IATA strategy and what can be achieved if the relationships are right. Unfortunately, far too often, the relationship between airlines and governments is a poor one. And I worry that it is getting worse, especially in Europe.

The road to Copenhagen, Part 2

Following his invitation in May 2009, I met up with UN Secretary General Ban Ki-moon in New York. It was a great success. I had prepared well, talking through my strategy with Sergei Ordzhonikidze, Director General of the UN office in Geneva and Under-Secretary General of the United Nations. He made some important suggestions for my meeting, which brought home to me how essential it is to test the waters if at all possible.

On my visit to see Ban Ki-moon, I was accompanied by Paul Steele and Doug Lavin, IATA's US Director. We met with the UN's environmental experts beforehand, briefing them on our work to date and the strategy going forward. We were then ushered in to the former South Korean Foreign Minister's head-office, on the top floor of the UN building, taking a private lift to get there. It's a relatively small room, wooden-panelled with a large UN seal on one wall. It's far from impressive until you stop to think about the meetings that must have taken place, the conversations that have shaped the development of the world. Our meeting lasted nearly an hour and Ban Ki-moon, in his calm, deep-thinking manner, asked a lot of well-informed questions. He must have been happy with our answers as he called aviation a role model that other industries should follow. His appreciation was posted on the UN website and gave IATA's efforts a great boost.

Despite the upbeat mood and the Secretary General's public support, I was very concerned that December 2009's COP-15 at Copenhagen would end in failure. In fact, I predicted as much to my colleagues on the way out of the UN building. There were so many pictures of the Secretary

General shaking hands that it became clear how exposed he was. The Secretary General of the UN's environmental agency, the UNFCCC, Yvo de Boer, was another hindrance. He had made no attempt to broker a deal. He seemed more interested in mobilizing popular support among green organizations. It was just rabble-rousing, getting young people into crowds to shout for a green agenda without understanding the reality. I think he believed that the 120 or so heads of state in Copenhagen would be impressed and write him a blank check. I'm glad to say he couldn't have been more wrong. Out of the 30,000 people that went to Copenhagen, 20,000 were fierce environmentalists. There wasn't a meeting, there was a circus—and an out of control one at that. People queued for hours just to get in and debates went on until the early hours without any end result. It was a lost opportunity to progress, harming the environment, harming business. The resignation of the Summit President, Ms Connie Hedegaard, didn't help. Yvo de Boer resigned a couple of months after the Copenhagen event and disappeared from the environmental debate.

At least, IATA and ICAO played their cards right. I was involved in the transport session with President Kobeh of ICAO. The maritime sector was also involved and the difference between the shipping and airline industry couldn't have been more pronounced. IATA staff helped enormously. The likes of Patricio Sepulveda, Juan Carlos Villate and Adefunke Adeyemi were part of the Chile, Colombia and Nigeria delegations respectively. They were able to provide vital technical assistance and knowledgeable support at government sessions.

It was important information. We must have governments that are serious about both aviation and the environment. For example, only governments can make decisions about airspace. And the potential CO_2 savings in properly managed air traffic systems is huge. It is just one of several major issues that aviation partners must resolve to help airlines achieve their environmental goals.

Improving air traffic management

One argument about the environment came easy. CO_2 emissions are a result of fuel burn, and fuel is expensive. Airlines really don't want to spend any more on fuel than they have to—I think anybody can appreciate that, even the most ardent green supporters. So airline efforts to cut fuel are directly related to improving the environment. An IATA analysis of 144 airlines showed they managed a 5% increase in fuel efficiency in 2010 compared with 2009. This is on top of the huge improvements since the advent of the jet engine. As mentioned earlier, the engines today are close to 80% more fuel efficient than their 1960s counterparts. It is an ongoing campaign. There are a number of ways to be more fuel efficient and airlines are involved with them all. They have spent money on new engines and have taken weight off the aircraft. Passengers may not have noticed it but catering trolleys are lighter, seats are lighter, even the cutlery weighs less. In keeping with the modern world, weight became an obsession. IATA was the fitness coach, constantly challenging airlines and manufacturers to work hard to lose the extra pounds. And when we hit upon some new way to shave off another ounce or two, we shared the findings with all the membership through our dedicated teams, in particular with the smaller airlines that did not have the resources to spare for this kind of work.

Sharing operational efficiency improvements became commonplace through IATA's Go Teams, after called Green Teams. These teams were composed of pilots, flight dispatchers, engineers and air traffic controllers. They had been set up to assist airlines to improve their fuel efficiency and exchange best practices. On average, the assessments done by the Go Teams identified and validated around 10% in fuel saving opportunities. That's millions of tons of CO_2 emissions. The IATA Board of Governors didn't comprehend the effectiveness of the Go Teams immediately. Some 60 airlines had undergone the process by the time I had to advise our

Board members to support the service. Even here, among respected airlines, our Go Teams managed to make a difference, saving 2% to 12%. But the real difference was in the attitudes of the CEOs. Some accepted the Go Team visit openly, like Wolfgang Mayrhuber at Lufthansa, and talked about the numbers. Others wanted to be more discreet and there was one notable dissenter who didn't want to undergo the analysis at all. We promised we would keep GoTeam findings confidential if that was what the airline requested, but I can only assume the European CEO in question was apprehensive about the results. Or maybe he erroneously thought his airline was still the best in the business.

On top of the Go Team visits, IATA started a campaign called "Save a Minute", which, as its name indicates, was aimed at shortening every flight by one minute through better airspace design, procedures and management. We calculated this simple saving would reduce fuel consumption on a single flight by an average of 62 litres and CO_2 emissions by 160 kilograms.

But this is small change compared with the real big ticket item in fuel savings: let airlines fly on a route that gets them directly from A to B rather than force them to zigzag along air corridors and across checkpoints that add miles, time, fuel burn and CO_2 emissions to every journey. The service from Rome to Amsterdam, just as an example, is unnecessarily complicated. It sets an aircraft off across the Mediterranean heading for the South of France rather than straight up through Italy. Moreover, airlines should be able to take-off and land in a manner befitting 21st-century technology. There is no need for the levelling off, which was normal practice; climb to a certain altitude, stay there for a while and then climb some more. It's the same coming down to land and it was intended to improve safety. It worked well but then so did the telegram and black and white TV. Times change and the industry must change with them. Green departures and continuous descent approaches

(CDAs) should be the norm. Where this has been in use, over 32,000 metric tons of CO_2 have been saved in a single year at a single airport.

The barriers to CDAs and other performance-based navigation ideas are usually technical and financial. These can be tricky to solve but not impossible. Reduced Vertical Separation Minima (RVSM) took a few years to implement but is now in use throughout the world. It makes better use of the airspace available by reducing the vertical separation—something that can be done safely with technology. High-level route changes or working with entire airspace blocks is more difficult. Most often the problem is political as countries seem to think that implementation of a new system would force them to relinquish their sovereignty over their airspace. This isn't true at all. They are simply required to harmonize with neighbouring airspace blocks and update to modern avionics. So when we talk of a Seamless Asian Sky, that doesn't mean one owner. Every country still retains control of its airspace but the blocks are harmonized. Another problem is the military/civil airspace split, with the former keen on hanging on to old territories. This is what stops an aircraft flying up through Italy on the Rome–Amsterdam route. And once in a while the problem is technical as countries desperately need to upgrade old infrastructure.

I was personally involved in a lot of IATA's route enhancement efforts due to the political nature of the problem. The Pearl River Delta issue is a good example of how sensitive the issue could be. Mainland China has political leadership over Hong Kong and Macau and so it was difficult for the Special Administrative Regions to speed up any processes aimed at enhancing take-offs and landings in the area. But we knew that any approach to Hong Kong over Mainland China was 25 minutes longer than it needed to be. During the many meetings I had with the Civil Aviation Authority in Hong Kong and their counterparts in Beijing, I was able to make some headway and new routes were eventually opened. Informally, the two major routes were called IATA-1 and IATA-2 in appreciation for the role we played. These routes saved time, fuel and emissions for flights across Mainland China and into the Pearl River Delta, although the latter region still remained slower than we would have liked.

It was a long, tough process. One day, I was having lunch at the Ritz Hotel in Beijing with an old Chinese politician, remembering the days when I negotiated establishing an Italian pipes factory in Tianjin. I asked him why it was taking so much time to achieve results on air traffic management despite the role of the central government, which could take decisions without any consultation. Part of the answer, he said, lies in the complexity of the region and converting to international norms. Interestingly, he also pointed out that Hong Kong's special status is something that Mainland China is very keen to respect strictly, because the Chinese Government could one day offer the same type of status to Taiwan as part of a reunification process.

I've no idea whether the Chinese Government was, or is, considering this but it made me realize we had achieved something special and about as much as could be expected.

There were plenty of other meetings about getting new air corridors and most of the time our efforts were successful. ICAO, through my friend Dr Kotaite and his successor, Dr Kobeh, were always very supportive.

SES and NextGen

What really needs to happen is the harmonization of airspace. That means NextGen in the United States and a Single Sky in Europe. NextGen could save over 10 million metric tons of fuel by 2030, the equivalent of nearly 34 metric tons of CO_2. Estimating a fuel cost of $165 per barrel, it would save airlines $24.3 billion. Why the delay in implementation? And NextGen is moving quickly compared with the Single European Sky

(SES), which is 20 years-plus in planning and counting. SES was on the agenda back in 1991. I was Chairman of the Association of European Airlines and had organized a campaign for passengers to sign a card to send to their Ministers requesting a single European sky. It was a response to the long delays the industry had experienced that summer. Colin Marshall at British Airways was at first reluctant to embarrass his Minister but he eventually realized we had to do something. Ministers across Europe received thousands of these cards. Karel Van Miert at the European Commission was very unhappy with me and showed me a document that said SES would happen within five years. I'm still waiting.

Europe has a single currency but 34 air navigation providers. By 2030, SES would save 5.6 metric tons of fuel, 17.7 metric tons of CO_2 and $14.3 billion. Efforts to implement SES are painfully slow. Targets for ANSPs set by the Performance Review Board are very weak. The same governments that want to tax aviation for their environmental damage have delayed endlessly on projects that would bring about far greater environmental savings than any tax or trading scheme in existence. To be fair, this isn't so much a problem with the European Commission, which is keen to further the program, but with individual states who are still reluctant to modernize their airspace. We need tough targets and we need strong penalties for failure to meet these targets. Otherwise we will still be talking about SES in another 20 years. It is a joke—but not a very funny one for the environment.

Fuelling the future

Rivalling harmonized airspace management as a major development in environmental mitigation efforts are biofuels. If aviation is to halve its CO_2 emissions by 2050 compared to 2005, then biofuels will have a massive role to play. They have the potential to reduce the carbon footprint 80% compared with jet fuel.

Biofuels are simply fuels made from biomass such as camelina, jatropha and algae. The first two are hardy nuts adaptable to most environments and the third just needs a good dose of salty water. They are known as second generation biofuels and have put paid to the green contention that biofuels will make food prices soar because biofuel crops will take over arable land. Actually, rather than damage the world economy, biofuels offer potential employment to thousands of farmers in developing countries. And biofuels made from urban waste offer equally appealing benefits. Several airlines are now exploring this possibility with expert companies.

Technically, biofuels have been a challenge. Airlines certainly couldn't afford to replace all their engines so biofuels have to be "drop-in". That is, they have to work with existing technology and blend with normal fuel. We've managed to do just that and there are now commercial flights operating with biofuel. The other issue is financial. Biofuels have to be comparable in price to Jet A1 if we are to have widespread use. That hasn't yet happened. At the moment, airlines would double or triple their fuel bill if they operated on biofuels. Doubling the production capacity—easy enough in a young industry—would reduce unit costs 5–20%. But the commercialization process needs help. Big Oil has been terribly disappointing in this respect. They colour their advertising campaigns green but they have never focused on aviation biofuels, preferring the margins in other lines of business. Only Exxon has shown any interest. The industry environment strategy targets 4% biofuels by 2020, but this will be tough due to the lack of support from the oil suppliers. There are many small entrepreneurs that already make biofuels, but only Big Oil can guarantee distribution to the thousands of airports around the world. Naturally enough, an airline has to have reliable and extensive supplies and realistically the major players have to step in. More research also needs to be done. The main biofuel of the future may still be in a laboratory somewhere.

The Secretary General of the UNFCCC, Christina Figueras, who has brought a completely new approach to the sector involving all the participants, welcomes the development of second generation biofuels. She makes presentations around the world outlining her support. Despite this, biofuels still receive limited government attention. One reason is the power of Big Oil behind the scenes. At $100 or so a barrel, aviation pays the oil companies around $160 billion a year, with refinery margins of around $15 billion. That's big business that they would like to keep. Perversely, airlines are not seen as a major client though. So airlines pay big money for little attention.

Governments need to work with both carrots and sticks to give the fledgling biofuels industry the support it so richly deserves. The United States has passed legislation in support of the development of biofuels with programs led by the Air Force, the FAA, and the Department of Agriculture. The Obama administration has announced that the US Navy will provide the market with biofuels to support this new, alternative sector. The Navy and Marine Corps will partner with the Energy and Agriculture Departments and will share a $510 million investment over three years for the production of drop-in biofuels. Mexico has been an active player and Aeromexico, under the excellent leadership of Andres Conesa, is the first airline that followed up on my call to paint a plane in green and operate one flight on a specific route (in this case Mexico–Costa Rica) always powered with biofuel. This weekly service is as green as it can be. Lufthansa has also conducted a 1,200-flight test program using biofuels. The Hamburg–Frankfurt service used a 50% blend in one of its engines and saves about one ton of CO_2 per flight. Results from all of these flights have so far returned normal data, underlining the fact that there are no operational issues.

The European Commission (namely Vice President Kallas and Commissioner Oettinger) has initiated discussions on how to fund research and motivate companies to be more active in the development of biofuels. The economic situation doesn't help but unfortunately, the Environment Commissioner is really interested in the Emissions Trading Scheme (EU ETS), a program not supported by ICAO and which many have asserted violates the terms of the Chicago Convention and other generally accepted principles of international law.

EU Emissions Trading Scheme

The EC has finally bowed to rising international pressure to defer implementation of the ETS outside of Europe and give ICAO one more opportunity to coordinate an international solution to the carbon emissions of global aviation at its next triennial session in September 2013.

This is the correct decision and is part of a solution I have been proposing for some time. I started the battle against the EU ETS in February 2011. I met with John Mica, Chairman of the Transportation and Infrastructure Committee in the US House of Representatives, and we discussed passing a bill that would force US airlines to ignore the EU ETS. This stance has been backed up by the US Senate. I also met with Ministers of Transport in Russia, China and India. I told them that while many countries and organizations are working for a greener future, Europe was intent on keeping bankers happy.

I did not have to work hard to generate opposition to the EU ETS. The basic idea of the scheme was that any airline flying to or from Europe had to pay for their CO_2 emissions. Effectively, they had to buy carbon allowances. No problem there if the idea was implemented on a global basis. Achieving CNG will need positive economic measures; it is the fourth pillar of IATA's Four Pillar Strategy. But bizarrely, Europe insisted that airlines paid for their entire journey. So if Qantas flew in to London from Sydney, it had to pay Europe for all its CO_2 emissions—even those that they emitted over

Australia, over Asia, over the Bay of Bengal and so on. Why Europe thought this was fair is beyond me. It's against the Chicago Convention, ICAO principles and, I would imagine, quite a few other clauses in international law. Clearly, it challenges the notion of sovereignty. Not surprisingly, there were some strong opposition comments, most notably from the United States, China and India. The Court of Justice of the European Union came down in favour of the EU ETS after a legal challenge involving Airlines for America, The National Airlines Council for Canada, IATA and some US airlines. It said that the EU isn't a signatory to the Chicago Convention. Furthermore, the scheme only applied to aircraft taking off or landing in Europe, so it wasn't overreaching. Europe has similar laws, on safety for example, that aren't being questioned.

Not surprisingly, this interpretation did not satisfy other countries. Talks of a trade war intensified and those countries fighting against the EU ETS met together to announce their dissatisfaction. We could actually have got to a stage where US carriers could not fly into Europe. That would have been a complete nonsense in this day and age.

I started working on a solution after talking with EC Vice President Siim Kallas. After I left IATA, he offered me the job as President of ACARE (the Advisory Council for Aviation Research and Innovation in Europe). I appreciated the offer but I could not accept because Brussels is not the right environment for me. But I did promise to help find a way out of the emissions trading mess.

I presented my solution while I was receiving the Public Service Award from the President of the Republic in Singapore, Tony Tan Keng Yam, in February 2012. The idea is quite straightforward:

- *First, all the countries fighting against the scheme must recognize that Europe's intentions are good—that they have raised the bar on aviation and the environment.*

- *Second, Europe should limit the ETS to a regional scheme in 2013, suspend airline payments that are due in April 2013, and accept that ICAO is the right place to facilitate a global agreement.*
- *Third, Europe and ICAO must ensure that a global agreement is in place by the time of the ICAO Assembly in September 2013.*

A couple of months later, at the Aviation and Environment Summit in Geneva, my good friend, South Africa Tourism Minister Marthinus van Schalkwyk, also called for the Commission to suspend the international scope of the EU ETS.

I am very pleased that the European Commission listened. I believe my solution means there will be no losers, only winners. And the biggest winner of all would be the environment. I am strongly in favour of what ICAO has done so far and I am confident it will find a way to broker a global agreement. Most importantly, if airlines can buy permits from other sectors, then we won't have an explosion in prices that might result if airlines have to operate within aviation alone. ICAO could even add in IATA's targets on fuel efficiency so we are sure to get to carbon-neutral growth by 2020.

Europe has said all along that EU ETS was born out of frustration with the slow pace of ICAO's work. They have never denied that a global solution is preferable. Indeed, at the February 2011 Singapore Aviation Leadership Summit, Vice President Kallas said quite clearly that the issue "must be tackled, and solved, in ICAO. Of course, Europe wants to see a multilateral solution. And we are ready to battle for that outcome."

Let's hope that is true. If the EU could just spend as much political energy on the Single European Sky and supporting global schemes as it did on the EU ETS, we might actually get somewhere.

CHAPTER SEVEN
Safety First

Making the skies ever safer

Number one

Safety is the airlines' top priority. It always has been and always will be. In 1945, when IATA started, there were 9 million passengers and 247 fatalities. In 2012, nearly 3 billion people flew safely on 37.5 million flights. There were just 417 fatalities. Overall, there was one accident for every 5 million flights. It was the safest year ever. Every life lost is a tragedy, but in the industry we are proud that flying is the safest form of transportation.

The tireless work by IATA and airlines to keep raising the bar in safety is responsible for this incredible record. Anybody who thinks that airlines will cut corners in safety just to cut cost is wrong. Let's be clear— an accident is so costly that it would never make business sense not to be as safe as possible. So even if you think airlines are heartless (which they are not), accept the rational argument that safety is paramount because an accident could bankrupt the business.

Concerns about safety run through aviation history. It has been a crucial part of the industry since the Wright Brothers took to the air. In fact, when the first IATA was established in 1919, safety was the focus. IATA worked alongside the International Commission for Air Navigation (ICAN), which was founded the same year by the Paris Convention, to set the guidelines for the technical and operational standards for the fledgling industry. The 1944 Chicago Convention moved things on and ICAO became the responsible body for setting the technical regulations with the new IATA assisting on a practical level. On each step of the way, cooperation was the key. The impressive improvements made so far have stemmed directly from this approach. Safety cannot have political, economic or commercial boundaries.

Remember, governments originally gave IATA the responsibility to decide the price of air tickets because they did not want to compromise collaborative safety efforts by making the market a free-for-all. Airlines needed to work together and allowing a fare that gave carriers the opportunity to make a return and reinvest in better equipment was thought to be the best way forward. The United States eventually moved toward deregulation in the 1970s, but by then the market had matured and it was clear that airlines understood the need to be safe. Nobody gains from an accident—it dampens demand for the industry as a whole.

And of course manufacturers have played an important part in safety advances too. Every technological advance has made flying safer. And there have been plenty, from improved avionics to geared turbo-fan engines. In short, there really are no barriers. All safety-related information is shared openly and there is total transparency.

Handle with care

It is all very well talking about this openness and the desire to improve safety. But it was clear to me when I took over at IATA that there needed to be a formal approach, a focus on exactly what needed to be done. Regulators, while making the right noises about safety, had failed to hammer home the advantages of an industry consensus. A steady decline in their budget and relevant skills was becoming apparent. A lack of money was affecting the airlines too and many of them were flying old aircraft. Added to this was a high proportion of non-Western aircraft, a legacy of the old geopolitical environment. This didn't help matters because the old Russian jets still being flown weren't up to the same standard as a modern jet aircraft. In some regions, aircraft-worthiness certification seemed too easy.

I started to think about what IATA could do to raise the bar. I knew there was a genuine desire to improve but this was not enough. I also felt there was a little too much dependency on technical solutions. The reliability and sophisticated systems of modern turbine-engine aircraft means it is rare for an accident to have a strictly aircraft-related cause. So there needed to be a greater focus on the human elements of the systems. I'm not just talking about pilots. All areas of airline operations are a part of safety, from the top management down. I began to mould together a "big picture" perspective. I wanted a safety program that could be developed and applied universally to achieve genuine safety improvements. And it had to work whatever the size or the geographical location of the airline.

In 2000, the accident rate (measured as Western-built jet hull losses per million flights) was 1.2. I thought cutting this rate in half would be an achievable aspiration. As usual, I was told this was impossible as so much of the process was outside of the airlines' control. Also as usual I decided to ignore this advice. Finding the right role for IATA in the ongoing challenge to improve safety was essential. It wasn't just a case of fighting internally this time, however. In theory, I would be going up against civil aviation authorities, which, by law, were the only ones capable of making safety rules in their own territories and ensuring those rules were enforced. Battling civil aviation was not what I had in mind though. Too many of our member airlines had close links with their national authority and IATA too had formed close ties. Much of our work depended on the cooperation of civil aviation authorities. So the only way forward was to have them involved from the outset.

With the help of my Safety, Operations and Infrastructure team, several of the top civil aviation authorities were identified. These included the United States, Canada, Australia and the European Aviation Safety Agency (EASA). We asked these authorities to be involved from the start and follow the work step-by-step by playing a role in our steering committees. We made it clear from the beginning that this was an IATA program but their expertise was essential for the success of our program. Lots of meetings followed and eventually we were able to agree on some standards that we believed would help improve the safety process.

While this was going on it was becoming increasingly clear that certain countries faced a bigger challenge than others. Each of these countries had a different problem, however. In China and Russia, for example, despite the leadership of two very competent ministers—Yang Yuanyuan and Igor Levitin respectively—aviation had grown so quickly that civil aviation authorities had been unable to react fast enough. There was a string of accidents in both of these countries in the 1990s and early 2000s. In other countries, in Central Africa in particular, it was more straightforward. Simply, there was no safety oversight. The authorities there—if you can call them "authorities"—seemed to be actively against industry efforts, providing havens for all manner of airlines, some of them involved in illegal trade. The situation had become so serious that ICAO became involved and a number of internal meetings were held to address the problem.

Around this time there was an internal Boeing report. It worried that, because aircraft deliveries were increasing and new airlines were entering the market, that the hull loss rate would rise. It was a simple sum really. More flights meant more chance of an accident, especially with so many start-up, novice airlines. There is a tipping point to this equation. If there are too many accidents in any one year, the public demand for flights would be greatly reduced. There would rightly be an outcry about the safety of aviation. The Boeing document pointed out that it didn't matter that the increase in flights could mean it was a smaller hull loss rate than before. If there is an accident every month, would you be keen to fly?

So something had to be done. We couldn't put our number one priority at risk. I knew I had to make some strong decisions but I also knew I had to remember the message on the side of boxes with fragile goods inside: handle with care.

Beginning the audit process

I had to be careful because regulators are very sensitive about safety. In one sense they are right to be so because safety should always be a very serious issue. But on the other hand they are rarely experienced pilots or engineers. Their rulings sometimes reflect political sensitivities rather than deep industry knowledge.

As we had some civil aviation authorities working with us, I felt sure we could set up a team that could implement a new safety audit system without upsetting the regulators too much. This was an issue that needed everybody pulling in the same direction. Mike O'Brien was chosen as the Director for this project because more than any other candidate he had this balanced approach—a firm hand but a fair one. But it was Günther Matschnigg, Senior Vice President of IATA's Safety, Operations and Infrastructure division, who got the ball rolling by having a few, small meetings with select airlines. Air Canada, United Airlines and American Airlines were some of the carriers involved. It is no surprise the Americans were interested in the idea of a universal audit. In 1999, Swissair Flight 111 crashed off the coast near Halifax, Nova Scotia, at a place called Peggy's Cove. A fire on board had become uncontrollable. It had become apparent that a lot of passengers were issued tickets by Swissair's codeshare partner, Delta Air Lines. These passengers didn't know they were flying on a non-US airline. The FAA had moved to ensure that US carriers were required to enhance significantly their safety audit of foreign codeshare partners. So the US carriers reasoned that a new auditing process would be of great assistance to them in handling FAA requirements.

The FAA regulations also highlighted the challenge we faced. There was no consistency in standards, no required experience for the auditors and very limited quality assurance processes. There were just rules—and plenty of them. And the even bigger problem was the fact that security had taken over the agenda. Since 9/11, regulators had become convinced that security issues were the industry's top priority. A new safety audit based on common standards was put on the backburner.

The main players

I didn't want the momentum to fade though. Some good work had been done and IATA had a tool in place, the Operational Safety Audit (IOSA), that seemed to me to be the perfect vehicle for our new safety program. But we needed a strategy, a roadmap to transform an idea into a viable tool, one that could mark a major breakthrough in the industry's safety efforts.

I talked about this a lot with my great friend, ICAO President Dr Assad Kotaite. We discussed the idea of a safety audit extensively, focusing on how it could work in a practical sense. ICAO was behind many of the existing safety programs and I learned a lot. But this time, ICAO was the starting point and not the finishing line for an IATA initiative. We talked further with the Americans and Europeans about what a good safety audit would look like. The new process had to be comprehensive. One element was pure ICAO, however. Because the system had to take into account all carriers, we needed to construct the audit in such a way that there would be areas that were mandatory and others that were optional, that would only apply according to the size of the fleet or type of aircraft. So ICAO continued to play an important role and Dr Kotaite was instrumental in setting the right framework for the project.

The ICAO audit—the Universal Safety Oversight Audit Program (USOAP)—had been established in 2001 to allow ICAO to check on its contracting states. Countries always have ultimate responsibility for carriers registered in their territory, but either through neglect or inexperience, many failed to ensure safety levels were adequately maintained. It wasn't so much that safety was jeopardized but more that the proper documentation was lacking. In this line of work there has to be a very detailed record. It may be vital should an incident occur.

Marion Blakey, the newly-appointed Administrator for the FAA, was another key player. The FAA was crucial to the success of the project. No other authority had their resource and skill levels. Marion was on board with the idea from the start. We developed a personal friendship and she took the trouble to visit me in Geneva to discuss better ways to cooperate. Very quickly we established that there was no conflict with existing FAA and ICAO safety regulations. The way was open for a comprehensive airline program. IATA had to step up.

Devil in the detail

The big picture was looking very promising but the practical details still had to be decided. How big should the audit be? How many auditors would be needed and in which disciplines? How much would an audit cost? Who would pay for it? This was a major undertaking and we needed clear answers.

By the beginning of 2003 we had pre-tested some of the standards and the results and methodology had been vetted by an Advisory Group. At the next Board meeting I updated the members on our progress. It was very informal. We always say that safety is the number one priority, so this was in a sense a very straightforward plan, one that was in keeping with the traditional priority of all our members.

Of course, in the aftermath of 9/11, cost was also a priority. I had been cutting the IATA workforce, so the main question I had to answer was how to implement a new audit while keeping our structure slim and our costs down. I decided the best way to go about this was to contract out the actual audit process to accredited organizations. In 2003, the first two companies were accredited—Aviation Quality Services and United Pros. Later that year, Qatar Airways became the first airline to be registered with the new-look IOSA.

The pricing of the audit turned out to have a simple solution despite the seeming difficulty of the challenge. A direct negotiation between an audit organization and an airline seemed to me to be counterproductive. It could potentially affect the accuracy of the audit and that couldn't be allowed. Nor could the audit cost too much. Smaller airlines with limited resources needed this audit at least as much as the larger airlines and I didn't want lack of money to act as an excuse. So in the end I decided that IATA, in the initial stages, would pay, regardless of the size or financial situation of the airline. We had extra revenue coming in through the expansion of our commercial services and this seemed to be the best way we could use the money. Safety, after all, is the top priority. Needless to say, this was very well received by the airlines. Not only did they get to be safer—they got to be safer free of charge.

While I had them in this state of mind, I implemented the next phase of my strategy: targets. These never went down well but hitting the target button was essential to a business approach. It's a recipe for success. Targets make the difference to any strategy. In any case, my insistence on targets was now expected by the Board. And in turn I expected an internal battle on what those targets should be. I was not disappointed.

A maybe to a must

I started discussing our goals with Robert Milton, CEO of Air Canada and Chairman of IATA at the time. Leo van Wyck and Jean-Cyril Spinetta, CEOs of KLM and Air France respectively, were also heavily involved. I suggested making the IOSA Registration mandatory for all IATA member airlines and a precondition for any airlines wishing to join IATA. While the notion of pushing safety as much as possible was acceptable, tying it to IATA membership was thought to be a step too far. It was argued that some airlines would lose the benefits of IATA membership because they could not afford to make all the changes necessary to pass the audit or because they would fail on some small technicalities. In other words, the association was turning its back on those members that needed it most. To stop this argument in its tracks I had the idea of a special fund for deserving airlines called Partnership for Safety (PfS). This would ensure that an airline had all the necessary help, financial or otherwise, to meet the exacting standards of IOSA. PfS consisted of seminars, targeted training courses and specific help from relevant experts. The IATA Training Fund (IAFT) also contributed to the PfS program. Over 100 airlines in many parts of the world benefited from PfS, and many attribute their ultimate IOSA success to the support they received through the scheme.

Even so, Board discussions about IOSA were not plain sailing. More than once I was told that we would lose all our African members or that regional airlines would choose not to undergo the audit. There were suggestions that a significant percentage of airlines would drop out of the association. I didn't want to talk about numbers though. I knew that a limited number of airlines might not make it, but I personally met with as many of the borderline carriers as I could, explaining and providing the resources that would help them meet IOSA standards.

Finally, at the 2006 Paris AGM, the following was announced:

- *Members had to plan an audit by end-2006.*
- *That audit had to be conducted by end-2007.*
- *All audit findings had to be closed and the airline on the IOSA Registry by end-2008.*

Failure to meet these goals would mean the airline would lose IATA membership. The time for talking was over. Airline CEOs had to show that safety was indeed at the top of the agenda and ensure their companies passed IOSA.

In the end, we lost 21 members. Some of those that failed initially have now passed IOSA and rejoined IATA. Crucially, from the beginning of 2009, all IATA member airlines had passed the most stringent and comprehensive safety audit. There were more airlines than that on the IOSA Registry though. As the program gathered strength over the first few years, it had become an accepted part of the industry safety efforts. Even non-member airlines were keen to undergo the audit to prove that they also held safety in the highest regard. IOSA also helps enormously with insurance premiums. IOSA not only made the skies safer, it made them cheaper too.

With airlines showing strong support, I started travelling extensively to promote IOSA with Civil Aviation Authorities and with Ministers of Transports. Although I talked mainly about IOSA being an airline tool, there was clearly an advantage in a country making IOSA a national requirement. I explained this would support ICAO's work. If every home airline was IOSA-registered then complying with USOAP would be a formality, a natural extension of aviation safety efforts.

Bit by bit, IOSA was gaining momentum. But the big breakthrough came when I received a call from the Egyptian Minister of Transport, General Shafik. A former military man, he had done a great job with civil aviation, and in so doing, made a huge contribution to Egyptian tourism. I had met him previously. I was on vacation in Cairo but agreed to a meeting while I was there. It didn't go exactly as planned because we got on so well the meeting went on for most of the morning. He isn't at all what you would expect from a five-star General and knew as much about the commercial side of aviation as he did about the technical side. That meeting was the start of a fruitful cooperation between IATA, the Ministry of Transport and Egyptair. The home airline was getting better all the time under the guidance of Eng. Atef, who was leading his own revolution at the carrier.

General Shafik's phone call was about the investigation into the crashed Flash Airlines plane that had gone down in the Red Sea, killing 148 people. He was worried that all his good work would be undone by the resulting stories and so he asked for an IATA team to go to Egypt immediately to present on IOSA. He wanted it made mandatory for every carrier in Egypt and for every carrier flying to Egypt. It was a good meeting and in due course, Egypt became the first country to make IOSA a national requirement. Not long after, Egyptair joined Star Alliance. I remember it well because I had suggested the move to Wolfgang Mayrhuber and Eng. Atef. Wolfgang was hesitant because he thought Africa was covered by South African Airways and Eng. Atef wasn't sure his carrier was ready. But somehow they made it happen. Egyptair threw the most fantastic party in the desert to celebrate, with the pyramids as a backdrop.

Because of the special relationship we enjoyed with the authorities and airline in Egypt, IATA had chosen Cairo to host its 2011 AGM. Unfortunately, the Arab Spring was on the horizon and Egypt was among the first to witness the revolutionary fervor. We had no option but to cancel and I had to call General Shafik, who had been appointed Prime Minister by Mubarak following the Egyptian uprising, as well as Eng. Atef, who had become Minister of Transport. It was a shame we couldn't reciprocate the magnificent support Egypt has shown for IATA programs. I hope that one day IATA will again consider Cairo as a venue for its AGM.

A meeting at the Kremlin

With the Egyptian mandate, IOSA had become a national tool as well as an airline one. My next target was Russia. Russia's problem was the large number of small airlines (nearly 100) still flying old Soviet-era aircraft. These were affecting the hull loss rate and damaging the perception of Russian aviation. I raised this point during a very interesting meeting with President Medvedev in November 2009 at the Kremlin. The meeting was organized by Igor Levitin, the Minister of Transport, and the man who has really transformed Russian aviation. Without him, there wouldn't be electronic ticketing in Russia and the safety record would be a lot worse. Minister Levitin supported me in all IATA projects and we became great friends in the process.

We arrived for the meeting with President Medvedev at the Kremlin in a minibus. I was with Minister Levitin, the US Secretary for Transport, Ray La Hood, and three European Ministers of Transport. The Red Square is very impressive, with red brick framing Lenin's Mausoleum and Saint Basil's Cathedral. Then, as you enter the big courtyard at the Kremlin you have the impression of a medieval citadel, complete with churches, administrative buildings and huge reception halls. You can imagine the many fine events this building has hosted but you are also left in no doubt about the communist history as there is a modern, concrete structure inaugurated by Khrushchev in 1961 to hold the Communist Party Assembly.

The first problem on the agenda was to solve Secretary La Hood's missing passport. He had forgotten it and so was having a problem getting through the strict security check. I had to rush up a wonderful marble staircase to ask Minister Levitin to solve the issue. Walking through the corridors at the Kremlin is an amazing experience, not only for the incredible statues, furniture and decoration, but also because you can almost hear the conversations from history, from Tsars to Cold War politics.

President Medvedev met us in a large, round meeting room and greeted us all personally. He showed a great grasp of aviation and had obviously studied his dossier well. He spoke for about 20 minutes without notes and summed up the Russian aviation situation perfectly. He expressed his appreciation of the role IATA had been playing in improving the safety and efficiency of the industry. I asked the President to support the e-freight program, explaining the benefits it would have for the business and security.

When talk turned to safety, I suggested making IOSA mandatory in Russia and giving the small airlines financial assistance. Although we didn't quite get that far, I did agree to translate the complete IOSA into Russian. I have had many similar meetings to this one but I have to say President Medvedev was one of the most impressive leaders. He had a very formal manner but was very professional and elaborated on his points with great clarity. He immediately grasped all aspects of a particular argument. The positive atmosphere generated at the meeting meant that safety was vigorously pursued at all levels of Russian aviation.

It's strange to think of the number of airlines in Russia because everybody still thinks mainly of Aeroflot. The reason for this is that it was once the biggest airline in the world, flying 120 million passengers every year. It had a fleet that was equal to the largest American carriers combined. Aeroflot is also one of the oldest airlines. It was founded in 1923 following a study on air transport that was signed by Lenin. Aeroflot started modernizing under the leadership of Vladimir Tikhonov in the late 1980s and early 1990s. I knew him quite well during my Alitalia days and I clearly remember the ceremony in 1989 when Aeroflot officially joined IATA. A huge delegation entered the meeting room at the start of the meeting, which was very impressive. It was a big day for IATA, too, because until then it had been perceived as a Western association. Aeroflot joining the Board sent a strong political statement.

One day, Tikhonov called me in my position as Chairman of the Association of European Airlines and told me he had a major problem and asked for my assistance. A meeting of the European CEOs had been planned for the weekend, so I invited him to join us in a small Italian town called Gubbio. I then invited Günter Eser, IATA Director General at the time, and organized a private meeting for the three of us at the end of the weekend. I thought if I can't help Tikhonov then surely Günter can. But when the Aeroflot CEO told us the problem, we were stunned. "The USSR is breaking up," he said. "And I have lost control of the airline. When an Aeroflot plane lands in a distant part of the USSR, it is being captured and used by the region to start its own airline." We didn't know what to say and of course couldn't offer any concrete help. But we said we would remain vigilant.

The next day Vladimir and I visited the Basilica of Assisi, where people from all religions come to pray for a better world. I didn't take him there on purpose but it does seem appropriate now. Eventually, Valery Okulov became CEO and transformed Aeroflot into a successful modern business. His successor, Vitaly Savelyev, has continued the good work. Aeroflot now flies Airbus and Boeing aircraft and has excellent customer service and an excellent safety record.

I returned to Russia shortly before I left IATA. Minister Levitin had organized a meeting attended by all the top people in Russian aviation. It was a kind gesture and he gave me a big picnic case as a leaving present. I have got a lot of use out of it while relaxing in the wonderful Swiss countryside. My final remarks to him were on safety. I proposed giving the smaller airlines two or three years to rid themselves of old aircraft and again called for financial assistance for them. I said the credibility of Russian aviation was at stake, especially as a new regional Sukhoi jet was coming to market. The day after this meeting I attended the La Bourget Air Show at the invitation of Jean Paul Herteman, the visionary Chairman and CEO of Safran, the maker of the successful CFM engine. I had lunch with my colleagues on the Safran Board and then went to visit Vitaly Savelyev at the Russian chalet. President Putin was there and clearly not in a good mood. A Yak-Service Yakovlev Yak-42 plane had crashed that morning in Northern Russia, killing many members of a Russian ice hockey team. In total, Russia had 15 accidents during 2007–11. And in 2012, a Sukhoi Superjet-100 crashed in Indonesia. Clearly, the country still has some work to do.

A dangerous traffic jam

Another country where IATA played a huge role in was Nigeria. It's a big country with a sizeable population and significant oil reserves, yet it hadn't ever paid much attention to aviation and aviation safety in particular. In 2005, a Bellview Airlines Boeing 737 crashed, killing 117 people. I wrote a letter of condolence to the President of Nigeria, explaining IATA's emphasis on safety and offering to help. I received a formal letter in reply but there was no follow-up. Soon after, in 2006, an ADC Airlines Boeing 737 went down with several dignitaries on board, including the son of a former President. It was the 11th accident in the country in just over ten years. This time there was a follow-up and IATA began working with Harold Demuren, the new Head of Nigerian Civil Aviation, and a man who worked day and night for several years to improve aviation safety in the country.

A new Minister of Transport, Diezanni Allison-Madueke, also played an important role. I met her at an ICAO Assembly not long after she became the Minister and she was instrumental in helping to set up a new IATA office in Lagos. She was a former Executive Director of Shell Nigeria and is now the Minister of Petroleum. I often meet her at Davos at the World Economic Forum where she is an active participant and we always talk about the old times and aviation.

I planned to visit our new office in early 2007, flying to Lagos from Madrid. Just before I left the Spanish capital, I had a breakfast meeting with Iberia CEO Fernando Conte and he told me to be careful in Nigeria because only a few days before an Iberia manager had been shot in his car on the way from the airport. I expressed how sorry I was to hear the news but didn't pay too much attention to the warning. I had often visited so-called dangerous countries and risk was part of the job.

I changed my mind very quickly, however. On arrival I learned I was to be guarded during my entire trip by a group of specially-trained Presidential soldiers. Apparently, the authorities had gathered intelligence that there was a threat on my life as IATA's strong position on the enforcement of security and safety regulations was threatening the illegal trade in arms and drugs. At the hotel I discovered I had been given the entire top floor, which was easier for the troops to secure. Every so often, even during the night, I was told to change rooms so my exact location couldn't be pinpointed. About 20 armed soldiers watched over me, some sleeping on the floor of my room. Anybody who came to see me, even my own staff, had to be searched.

All the journeys in the city were conducted at high speed in a convoy of six armed, bulletproof vans. The roads of Lagos, usually very busy, were cleared so my group of vehicles could get directly to the destination without stopping. My Corporate Communications Director, Tony Concil, couldn't get used to this, although I must admit it was worse for him because he was always told to travel in the first minivan. He was at the front of the action.

On my final day there, we held a press conference for about 100 journalists. Tony was very busy, so he excused himself from my final appointment at the local airline. This meeting wasn't planned and so the route through the city hadn't been cleared in advance. A few minutes into the journey we stopped suddenly.

And then the shooting started.

I was pushed to the floor of the van and my guard started shouting into the radio. I heard car doors slam and people running and screaming. The gunfire carried on and I started to get very scared. After several minutes the shooting stopped and I was allowed up from the floor.

When I asked what had happened, I couldn't believe the answer: a traffic jam! Because we were forced to stop, the soldiers started shooting in the air as a way of getting the cars to move out of the way. But everybody had become so scared that they had abandoned their cars and run away leaving us stuck in the middle. It wasn't a pleasant end to the trip but I can laugh about it now.

Accidents still happen of course. But we are learning all the time. Thanks to the great efforts of all the authorities involved, safety is improving. We also have to thank the efforts of centres of learning such as Cranfield University. Its School of Engineering is studying aircraft design and many other aerospace issues with great attention to detail. It has a dedicated course and a large part on accident investigation that helps explain what to do should an accident occur.

As for IOSA, it now has over 300 registered airlines and the number of countries that have mandated it at the state level is increasing all the time. There is no doubt that the audit has made a difference to IATA members and to aviation in general. Numbers tell the story. In 2012, no IOSA carrier had a Western-built jet hull loss accident. For the period 2002–11, there was a 58% improvement in safety. It is an incredible result. IATA achieved this by working with commitment and passion and utilizing the skills of the many aviation stakeholders.

CHAPTER EIGHT
Bad People, Not Bad Objects

The need for more efficient and harmonized security

A knee-jerk reaction

Like safety, security is an essential building block of modern aviation. And again, like safety, the industry has been able to raise the bar ever higher on security. But the similarities stop there. Security has a very different story to safety.

The key to success with safety was the team approach. The sharing of information and the sense of camaraderie that prevails in aviation safety is the result of the pioneering spirit that gave birth to this great industry. It's understood that all airlines can learn from each other when it comes to safety and no airline will keep important safety information to itself. Sharing data makes everybody safer.

But this didn't happen with security post-9/11. And it's easy to understand why.

It was a normal, busy day at OPODO when the Twin Towers were attacked. With the entire OPODO team, I watched the plane fly into the second tower. It was truly shocking. I had seen those towers being built, having worked in New York in the 1970s. I used to count the floors being constructed whenever I walked to work on Wall Street. Every 20 floors there was a different colour marker, which made the task easier.

The terrible events of 9/11 were always going to evoke an emotional response, especially in the United States. But it was tough in London too. The close relationship between the United Kingdom and the Unites States meant that everybody in London feared their city could be next. I even took to walking to work rather than taking the London Underground. And at OPODO, as at many businesses, there was a huge impact on business. We were left to do the same job but with 10% less resources. Some of the staff had been with us less than a month and had even moved countries to take a job with OPODO, but we had no choice other than to let them go. It was a painful and frightening time for everybody.

But, of course, it was worse in the United States. They had been targeted, the attack had been on their soil, and it was very difficult for them to keep calm and take considered action.

A very vocal debate developed in the United States. The fact is that the information to stop the attacks had been available but it was too fragmented. More than ten agencies dealt with national security and a lack of coordination created a gap in the system. The United States was spending billions of dollars to defend its country, but no agency was effectively handling the mass of information gathered in a consolidated effort to evaluate the risk and take appropriate counter-measures.

And remember, for the United States, flying was mass transportation, little different from the railways or greyhound buses. A passenger simply got on at one end of the journey and got off at the other. There wasn't much in place to improve upon. Sadly, it was all too easy for a terrorist to board an aircraft and use the aircraft as a weapon of mass destruction.

All this created trouble from the beginning. The United States wanted to change aviation security swiftly and decisively but it had enormous internal difficulties to overcome. And of course, what the United States decided would affect the rest of the world.

Admirals in the air

It took more than 15 months for the Bush Administration to build a new government structure that could lead and implement the many aviation security changes needed. The new department had to retake control of security for a mode of transportation that could no longer afford a romantic vision of flying. The first Secretary appointed to run the new Department of Homeland Security (DHS) was Tom Ridge in 2003. A former Congressman and Governor of Pennsylvania with no specific experience, he created an

Advisory Security System that just made the situation worse. Alarmingly, he didn't realize the difficulties and the panic that would be created should a day be designated "red". And all it meant was that the public should be vigilant. There were no plans to make security any different on red days. And they say some of my ideas are crazy!

Michael Chertoff took over from Ridge in 2005. A former judge and government legal heavyweight, he was the co-author of the US Patriot Act. He wasn't Bush's first choice, though. The former New York Police Department Chief, Bernie Korkik, was the first man nominated but had to decline the offer.

Chertoff started his tenure as Secretary of DHS with some startling ideas about lasers on board aircraft to defend against missile attacks. This was prompted by the Transportation Security Administration (TSA), the specialized branch of DHS dealing with transport security. At the beginning, the TSA was headed by an Admiral. Several times, while I was speaking with Admiral Loy and his successor Admiral Stone, we joked that most of our discussions were related to aviation but none of the US contingent had commercial or even military flying experience. Admiral Loy was a very competent man and I respected his input, but in the end I convinced the TSA to have some specific expertise from our industry joining the discussions.

The TSA has to deal with a lot of enquiries. But most of these calls are from Congressmen supporting companies more interested in selling some technology or other rather than addressing real risks. This is how Chertoff got the laser idea. It took the TSA valuable time to explain to the Congressmen and these companies that the risk of a plane being the target of a shoulder-launched surface-to-air missile was very remote. The risk assessment showed it would not be effective to equip commercial aircraft with the technology to defeat this threat. And anyway, a commercial plane does not maneuver like a fighter aircraft and would not be able to take advantage of the technology being used on military planes.

IATA created GASAG, the Global Aviation Security Action Group, to bring together all the major aviation players around common security positions. We needed to stop the really extreme views that were developing. The Group was successful in setting the tone for security policies on important issues like harmonization, funding and sky marshals. And we were also able to stop the US Visit Exit Program implementing the collection of fingerprints from travellers departing the United States. The idea would have forced airlines employees to perform a government role and the industry to bear the costs of the equipment, estimated at $12 billion. It wouldn't have been much fun for visitors either. I personally led the lobbying effort against the program, explaining at the Congress and government levels that this was not acceptable. We managed to put an end to this nonsense in summer 2008.

By this time, Chertoff had moved on to expanding the Advanced Passenger Information (API) program. API was creating a serious problem for many of our non-US members and in particular the EU airlines. The European CEOs had an impossible dilemma: if they provided the United States with the required information on passengers then they faced being prosecuted under EU privacy laws; but if they refused to release the information to the United States then they would be liable for a substantial fine every time they flew there.

I had to use all my diplomatic skills to broker a deal between Franco Frattini, the Vice President of the EC, and Secretary Chertoff. I explained that the airlines could not be exposed to this legal uncertainly and that a solution had to be found. Months of negotiations did not solve the problem, however. Just days before a self-imposed deadline there was still no solution on the table. I told my friend Frattini that both he and Chertoff had respected background experience as judges—so why not use that experience to find an instrument that could fit into the two legislations and solve the problem. It helped that they could fall back on their legal expertise rather than play politics and matters moved along swiftly after that. Just hours before the deadline, it was agreed that European airlines could send the passenger information. But a committee was formed to take care of "special cases", in effect creating a legal loophole.

It was a tough negotiation and it didn't make me optimistic about the future. But things changed for the better in 2009 when the Obama Administration appointed Janet Napolitano to the role as Secretary of the DHS.

My first visit to the new Secretary was very different from my previous meetings with the DHS team. She immediately understood that the concept of the former administration—"we decide, you implement" — could not work in a complex industry such as aviation. Finally, we had someone who understood that aviation's collaborative approach to safety could also work for security.

We first met at the old Marine Base Building, which looks like a bunker. But for once, aviation wasn't under fire from ridiculous government requirements. I gave Secretary Napolitano some examples of inconsistent requests from the US Administration and the confusing regulations sent to airlines by different offices of the same Department. The Secretary was very open and requested an explanation from her staff. A couple of months later many of the smaller problems were solved.

Secretary Napolitano brought a fresh approach to aviation security. She recognized that the threat and the industry are complex and global. More importantly, she understood that the industry and governments must work together. And it was not just words. I really felt it was the start of a new chapter in aviation security, a chapter that would produce many positive changes, an increased level of security and an end to passenger hassle.

But just as were starting to make real progress, in December 2009 a terrorist tried to get a bomb on board a US-bound aircraft from Amsterdam.

The Amsterdam incident

A passenger had boarded a Delta Air Lines plane in Amsterdam, en-route to Detroit. He had sown a bomb into his underwear that fortunately failed to detonate. He was tackled and held down by another passenger while the plane was landed safely.

The joy of a safe landing was short-lived. There was no escaping the fact that the system had failed miserably. A bomb had made it on board an aircraft.

I exchanged a lot of phone calls with the authorities in the United States and I was planning to fly to Washington to meet with Secretary Napolitano to offer IATA's assistance in any tightening of the system. As a matter of courtesy more than anything else, I invited Secretary Napolitano to Geneva to meet with myself and several of the senior airline CEOs. I was really pleased when she accepted the invitation and we quickly made arrangements for the meeting, which took place in January 2010.

I knew it would be a difficult discussion. That much was to be expected. What I didn't expect was the large number of requests from the US security forces regarding the logistics of the visit. I was planning to host a dinner at my villa, which is located in what is considered to be a good area of Geneva, near numerous consulates and diplomatic missions. Somewhat surprisingly, I was advised that because I had a large garden there was a risk and we should go elsewhere. That didn't fill me with confidence but we eventually settled on a nice chalet restaurant by Lake Geneva, near the United Nations. Of course, the establishment had to be inspected by the CIA and the Geneva police first.

The dinner was well attended. Secretary Napolitano and I were joined by some of the most prominent representatives of the Swiss Confederation government and many airline CEOs. The first course, a salad, was served and was very enjoyable. We all looked forward to the main course. But ten minutes later nothing had appeared. 20 minutes, 30 minutes…and still nothing. I started panicking and tried to attract the attention of my staff seated at the table, but everyone was involved in lively discussions. After some 50 minutes the main dish had still not arrived. But I caught glimpses of my very effective PA, Silvia Krahl, rushing up and down the stairs, signalling to me that all was under control. I always felt reassured when Silvia was dealing with something.

I asked what had gone wrong. Apparently there had been so many electronic devices fitted, including a scrambled, direct satellite connection to the White House, that the power had been drained from the kitchen and the meal had to be cooked elsewhere.

The White House connection was actually used during the dinner. Apparently there was a security alert in London and the Secretary had to discuss the US position with President Obama. It all made for a long dinner but I'm pleased to say that it ended up a positive one and we were able to build on the relationship the following day at the IATA offices.

Obviously a single meeting cannot solve every challenge, but a security roadmap was developed. We agreed to work together to ensure security measures could benefit from airlines' operational expertise; to aligning requirements with industry capabilities; and to getting governments to harmonize their approach across borders. We also agreed that a next generation security checkpoint would be necessary, one that could look for bad people and not just bad objects.

The real result was not the agenda but rather the new approach brought forward by President Obama and Secretary Napolitano. Combining government intelligence with airline operational expertise was the right way to go.

Trusting the shipper

In October 2010, there was another terrorist plot, this time using printer cartridges to get explosives aboard cargo carriers. Good information shared between different security agencies, notably those of the Saudi Arabians and the United States, stopped the incident in time—which shows how far aviation security had come since 9/11. But the plot was also an example of how vulnerable the air freight system is today.

Cargo is an important part of the air transport industry—it represents over $50 billion in revenue. Some 35% of total goods by value are shipped by air. Most of the high-tech components, microchips, automotive parts, TVs, medical components, medicines and high-class fashion are transported by air. Much of it is part of a "just-in-time" production and delivery model crucial to many businesses. If the system stops, the world stops. We experienced that during the Icelandic volcano eruption when many factories had to close due to the lack of spare parts.

The reason air cargo is so vulnerable is simple—there is no technology available today that can effectively scan a large cargo container. And it's near impossible to unpack the container to scan single packages because the time and space that would require would gridlock the entire air freight system. It would probably cause some major delays for passenger flights too.

To mitigate the risk the shipper evaluates the origin of a shipment. Did it come from a trusted company, one that has sent shipments before and has declared all the required information? This is the basis of cargo security today. Given that we cannot scan entire containers and that we cannot afford to unpack them, it is the sensible way forward. IATA is playing a big role in ensuring the robustness and harmonization of so-called known shipper programs. The association's e-freight program will be particularly important, doing away with an unreliable paper system and moving air cargo into the digital world. It started in 2009 and will need a couple of years yet to be fully implemented. It has taken longer than taking away the passenger ticket because it relies on freight forwarders to make the change rather than the airlines. But it will make a major difference to the entire cargo process, including cargo security.

Security costs

The United States' confusion after 9/11 has influenced government policy on aviation security for the past decade. For the most part, governments have pursued policies that have had little regard for the costs they impose on travellers and that fail to deliver on appreciable risk reduction. By 2010, a real patchwork of regulations around the world was costing airlines $7.4 billion. Inevitably, these costs are reflected in the higher cost of travel for passengers and higher costs for shippers.

Security costs don't stop there. The TSA alone spends around $5 billion manning walk-through metal detectors, overseeing baggage x-rays and conducting other screening activities. The National Aviation Studies Advisory Panel estimates that since 9/11 the TSA has spent $40 billion on screening passengers. And if these costs are extrapolated to airports worldwide, clearly vast amounts of money are being spent on a process that just seems to be getting worse in terms of the customer experience. Security queues are long and often intimidating. Throughput of passengers has dropped from an average of 335 passengers per hour prior to 9/11 to an average of 149 passengers per hour today. And every passenger is uniformly screened. Benjamin Franklin first said that time is money but he would have been shocked by exactly how much time and money has been wasted on aviation security.

The buffer time between arriving at an airport and getting on a flight has naturally been extended too. According to a survey by the Resources

System Group, the number of passengers arriving at an airport two or three hours before departure rose from 20% to 40% in the three years following 9/11. The number of passengers arriving just one hour in advance fell from 20% to 10%. The survey also revealed passengers travelling on business class would be willing to pay $70 extra to reduce travel time by one hour while other, less time-sensitive passengers on leisure trips and visiting friends would pay up to $31. Another study by Robert Poole of RAND calculates that the additional time spent waiting at the airport in the United States due to security procedures has cost passengers about $8 billion a year in the past decade.

In the United States, the economic and social cost of the failure of security measures does not end with air transport. Researchers at Cornell University found evidence that after 9/11 some travellers switched from flying to driving. They found that over 1,200 road traffic fatalities could be attributed to the impact of 9/11. Of course, this cannot be directly attributed to the added inconvenience caused by security measures. But it can be attributed to a fear of terrorism; a fear that the immediate security reaction by US authorities did not allay. This illustrates the unintended consequences of the failure of security measures.

The hassle for the passenger and the cost for the industry cannot be tolerated any longer.

Tomorrow's system today

Security has been improved since 9/11. But these improvements have come at a very high price, financially and in terms of the passenger experience. And the fact is that air traffic continues to grow. There is no way the security system in place today can cope with the needs of tomorrow. I would argue that the system is already failing. At thousands of airports around the world, passengers are being hassled, confused and intimidated. Should belts and shoes stay on, should the laptop come out of the bag? It is a one-size-fits-all approach.

Technology is an important part of the solution. We are not speaking about rocket science here, just improving the current system or speeding up some existing technologies. I believe that too many companies have got lazy in recent years and are not putting in the necessary effort to find new products. The existing products are selling well and selling for a premium. There is no need to put out version 2 when version1 is still a hot seller.

We need a security experience that is effective, efficient and convenient for countries, airlines and airport operators. IATA's idea of searching for bad people and not just bad objects is predicated on the proactive use of intelligence data, combined with new technologies and harmonized throughout the world. I had been working on this concept for some time as it was clear that governments were not going to seek global solutions without IATA's assistance.

The main problem I had was finding someone with the necessary skills to be the IATA Director of Security. The position requires someone with an aviation background to interface with his airline counterparts. But, post-9/11, we also needed some added value. There needed to be experience in the security agency system and an understanding of future technological trends. Most of all, the person had to have the willpower to drive change.

The manager I inherited at IATA didn't have the right profile. I looked around for his replacement but could not find anyone in the industry. So I extended my search to respected security agencies with recognized international experience. I appointed a former high-ranking officer of the Canadian Mounties, but he did not fit into the job. Aviation is like a club and if you have not been a part of it, it can be difficult to adapt, to understand the culture and gain the respect necessary to lead the 240 or so IATA member airlines.

I then appointed another important expert in security, this time with a background in intelligence in a major European country. He had also held a top job at one of the top European multinational companies. Again, however, the chemistry did not work. The role needed his technical knowledge, but when you're dealing with governments at a very senior level, you also need great diplomatic and negotiating skills. There was an amicable parting of the ways and IATA certainly gained from the knowledge that this person brought to the IATA team.

I could not afford failure for a third time. I started looking internally and, as on many other occasions, the best placed person was indeed already working for IATA. I had hired Ken Dunlap in 2005 as Director of Security for North America. He later took on the global position. He had worked for United Airlines as a pilot and was then involved in security issues within his airline and with the House Foreign Affairs Committee. Ken has done a great job and will play a vital role in improving the security process for passengers and government in the years ahead.

Ken was instrumental in following up on Secretary Napolitano's visit to Geneva in January 2010. During her visit, I told Secretary Napolitano that we needed to find a way to meet security requirements that doesn't involve a horrible experience for the passenger. I followed up on this by visiting experts and exchanging views with manufacturers in the major technical areas. A visit to Israel was very useful in evaluating new technologies and the latest in behavioural analysis techniques.

I started working with Ken and initially we asked what the passenger wanted. Our answer was a process that was fast and uncomplicated; no undressing, searching pockets for keys and coins, putting miniature toiletries in a clear plastic bag and so on. Thinking about this, we recognized that a one-size-fits-all process was never going to achieve this goal. As it stood, the security checkpoint had to assume the worse of everybody. So we started wondering about how to differentiate between passengers. We needed to separate the frequent flyer with masses of personal information available with the passenger for whom there were no records and who had paid cash. It was the beginning of yet another "crazy Giovanni idea".

Airlines had information available on their passengers but this wasn't enough. We needed to integrate this with national security agencies and cross-profile with criminal records. We believed we had a good concept. The security process of the future needed to differentiate between passengers so that resources could be allocated efficiently. And this would mean working with all the information available, from airline frequent flyer schemes through to data held by security agencies.

From a passenger point of view, he or she will send all required information prior to the flight. If she is a member of a frequent flyer scheme, much of this information is already stored. Then, at the airport, she will approach the security area and present her documents to a machine or an officer. Her information will be processed and within seconds she would be directed to one of three lanes. All she will have to do then is walk through the lane, which would be less than ten metres long, and into the departure lounge. Technology will screen her as she walks along the lane, verifying identity and scanning for any unacceptable items. If she is directed toward the "higher-risk" lane then she would have to walk slower as the scanning took place. If there is still an issue there will be additional procedures and perhaps personal screening in a booth. The whole process will usually take less than a minute, and frankly, it is the only way aviation security will be able to handle more than 3 billion airline passengers a year. By 2030, we're anticipating some 16 billion passengers a year. If we carry on treating everybody as high risk, which is what happens at the moment, then soon enough the security queues would trail out to the parking lot.

Coming up with the idea of a Checkpoint of the Future (CoF) was the easy part. The hard part was how to make this happen. We had taken some important steps before I retired. At my last AGM as Director

General of IATA in Singapore, we had a display of the CoF concept and I had won several important acknowledgements that this was the way forward. The European Commission, the Chinese government, the US Department of Homeland Security, Interpol and a number of countries all expressed support for the CoF project.

How quickly we get to the CoF from here depends largely on the governments. To begin with, they must put pressure on manufacturers to come up with the technology necessary to screen a moving target. That means stopping the enormous sums of money governments are spending on current technology. Only when manufacturers' healthy profit margins are threatened will they start serious work on producing a next generation of scanners. The basic technology is there so I'm confident we can solve the technical issues quickly.

I think the toughest part of the concept is getting governments to agree on the data needed to assess a passenger properly. What will make the US government feel safe enough to direct a passenger toward the low-risk lane? Governments around the world don't necessarily have to harmonize. The CoF will present a menu of options so the authorities can choose the package that is right for them and for the airport. Even so, there does need to be mutual recognition of risk assessment systems and this will take a lot of talking and some skilful negotiations.

Checkpoint of the Future has adopted a three-phase strategy. By 2014, existing technologies and processes will be adjusted to pave the way for a risk-based concept. By 2017, biometric identification and known traveller programs should be mature enough for differentiation in passenger screening to become quite common. Finally, by 2020, unobtrusive screening—walking through a lane without stopping—should be a reality.

Getting security right is vital to the future sustainability of the industry. Passengers appreciate that flying is quick, relatively cheap compared with other modes of transportation and very, very safe. But the hassle at the security checkpoint means many people aren't fond of flying. So improving security would have a real impact on the relationship between the passenger and the airline. While security is a problem, airlines will find it hard to win passenger support. But if aviation can solve this problem then it will regain a lot of credibility in the eyes of the public. This will go a long way to counteracting the negative policies of so many governments. This is in addition to the obvious operational efficiencies an improved security checkpoint would bring. So with one shot, aviation could achieve two great results.

At the 2012 Davos World Economic Forum, Secretary Napolitano, who is a strong supporter of the Checkpoint of the Future, said to the audience, "It's time to take away the 'Future' and just call it 'Checkpoint of Today'." Coming from such a prominent member of the US government it points to a brilliant future for the CoF.

I also spoke at the 2012 Davos World Economic Forum. As Chairman of the Aviation, Travel and Tourism Council, I presented a new e-visa project that was also presented to the G20 Summit in Mexico. Imagine a future that did away not only with a very unpleasant security experience but also with all the paperwork involved in getting the right stamp in your passport even before you fly. What the travel experience needs to achieve is the subject of the last chapter.

CHAPTER NINE
Vision 2050

A look at Vision 2050, liberalization
and thoughts on the future

The need for change

My biggest problem throughout my decade at IATA was that the industry desperately needed a new set of rules. We were being run by the same system that was in place when the DC-3 was flying.

The 1944 Chicago Convention put safety at the top of the agenda and we owe a lot to the visionary 52 states that first signed the Convention. It put civil aviation back on track after the tragedy of the Second World War. But Article 6 of the Convention stated that no scheduled international air service may be operated over or into the territory of a contracting country, except with the special permission or other authorization of that country. Prior to that, airlines didn't need an act of Parliament to open a route. And foreign ownership was not unusual. SCADTA, for example, which would ultimately become Avianca, was owned by Germans.

The Chicago Convention was followed by the Bermuda Agreement in 1946 in which the United Kingdom and the United States agreed to a bilateral deal. There used to be regular 32-hour trips across the Atlantic with the famous Boeing 314 flying boats, but the United Kingdom—conscious that the United States was a growing power— pushed to regulate traffic. So the bilateral system was born and the concepts of government-regulated capacity and of national ownership became the norm. The problem is these rules are still largely in place even though the world has changed so much. Airline hands are tied. All they can do is adapt as much as possible within the framework set by governments.

The Latin American model

The best examples of how airlines have adapted come from Latin America. Look at the Chilean carrier, LAN. Like a few other carriers, its leadership has had the courage and vision to push governments to accept "clone" airlines. This strategy gave us the likes of LAN Argentina, which began business in 2005, as well as LAN Ecuador and LAN Peru. These are subsidiaries of LAN but work around foreign ownership rules.

Apart from great leadership, part of the reason this business model has been accepted is that many Latin American governments understand the impact of the failure of a national carrier. There have been some painful lessons in the Latin American region that must not be forgotten by the industry.

In 2001, Aerolíneas Argentinas was suspended from IATA's financial systems because of the airline's many problems. The government knew the news was coming and held a cabinet meeting to re-nationalize the airline immediately. I travelled to Buenos Aires a number of times to assist its President, Mariano Recalde, in restructuring the airline. At the end of this process, I also often met with President Cristina Fernández, who had assumed office after the presidential period of her husband, Nestor Kirchner. Unfortunately, he died just two years later. Her Presidential residence at Olivos was an amazing villa about 30 minutes outside of Buenos Aires. It had wonderful gardens, impeccably manicured and home to an incredible variety of brightly-coloured plants. We had a meeting there in 2010 to celebrate the fact that the airline was once again a full member of IATA's financial systems and we chatted about the challenges ahead for the industry. Although she was charming, I could see she was distracted. She said she was due to give a big speech later that day to present officially her candidacy for the next elections. The opposition had been gaining according to the polls and she had to make an impression with her speech or she might be in trouble. I escorted her to her helicopter that was taking her to the soccer stadium where the rally for her political party was being held. I went back to my favourite hotel, the Alvear Palace, and with Patricio Sepulveda, IATA's Regional Vice President for Latin America, followed every word of her speech, delivered to some 60,000 people, on TV. Wearing as always an immaculate black dress, she spoke for over an hour without once appearing to refer to her notes. I told Patricio that she had done superbly and had the charisma of Eva Peron. She became the first woman ever to be re-elected in South America.

In Brazil, Varig hasn't been so lucky. It was founded in 1927 and although well-respected was basically hostage to its major shareholder, the Ruben Berta Foundation, which in turn was controlled by employee unions. These couldn't generate capital and wouldn't accept outside capital.

In the mid-1990s, Fernando Pinto—who moved on to become CEO of TAP Portugal in 2000—managed to reduce Varig's debt from $2 billion to $900 million. His leadership enabled him to reorganize the company enough to gain Star Alliance membership in 1997, but Varig was still ruled by committee with trade union employees in the driving seat. That's a challenge that even the most visionary and persuasive leader would struggle to overcome.

Pinto was followed by Ozires Silva, a former President of Embraer and Petrobas, and a Minister for Infrastructure. After him came Omar Carneiro Da Cunha, former CEO of Shell Brazil. Omar came to see me in Geneva to talk about the work he was planning to do in the airline. We had a constructive meeting and discussed the way forward for Varig, including all the restructuring problems caused by the Ruben Berta Foundation. We ended the day with a pleasant dinner where he realized that he had forgotten his mobile phone. I offered to get him another phone but he said as he was flying back the next day it wouldn't be necessary. I did, however, manage to persuade him to let my driver,

Enzo—IATA's oldest and most loyal employee—give him a tour of Lake Geneva in the morning before he flew back.

We said our goodbyes after dinner. But then, during the night, the IATA Brazil office called. They asked me to contact Omar urgently. I explained that it would be difficult as he didn't have a phone. I asked what the message was and received a very short reply: he had been fired. I could have got the message to him in the morning but when I called Enzo he said Omar was having a great time and really enjoying the natural splendour around the Lake. I decided against speaking with Omar as I wanted him to enjoy his day, free from the pressures of work for a while. I believe he got the news that he was out of a job when he arrived back, which is not the best way of saying "Welcome home".

A few years later, the situation at Varig had become so bad that I had to suspend it from IATA's Clearing House. It was during the 2006 World Cup in Germany. My decision was bound to cause some operational problems for the airline and in turn that would doubtless affect the many thousands of Brazilians who were in Germany supporting their team. Star Alliance partners made sure everybody got home but the writing was on the wall for Varig. The courts eventually split the airline into "new Varig" and "old Varig". The latter has disappeared while the former was purchased by Gol, a new breed of Brazilian airline that is serving this growing and enormously important market.

These are two examples of poorly managed airlines struggling to survive. But the turnaround in the region has been astonishing and it is not fully appreciated outside the industry.

Step by step, governments are beginning to realize the benefits of the "clone" airline approach. There is also a unique set-up in much of Latin America that is certainly helping governments to understand air transport. The CEOs of the successful airlines—such as LAN, TAM, COPA and Avianca—are major shareholders in their company and so take a medium to long-term view of the market. They don't get caught up in quick fixes that inevitably lead to escalating problems further down the line. Often, there is a family tie there that goes back 60 or 70 years. The Kriete family has a share in TACA, for example; there is the Mota family behind COPA and the De Oliveira's of GOL. Avianca has benefited from the leadership of Germán Efromovich. LAN was relaunched by Juan Cueto and his sons, Enrique and Ignacio, and they have built it up into a major success story, while TAM was the brainchild of the flamboyant Comandante Rolim Amaro. He was always surrounded by beautiful uniformed women but took a personal interest in everything, greeting passengers and establishing a department called "Talk to the President". Maurico and Maria Claudia Amaro, together with Enrique and Ignacio Cueto, were the architects of the merger between LAN and TAM. The LATAM Airlines Group, as the merger is known, is either the biggest or second biggest airline in the world by market value. Depending on how you measure these things, Air China may just about pip them to the post. LAN and TAM have been doing business for many years and the relationship has culminated in an airline that is a global powerhouse. Consolidation has worked wonders in Latin America and it would be successful elsewhere, too, if only governments would give airlines the chance.

This way of working isn't the only recipe for success by any means, but when used properly, this sort of network can be very powerful. The airlines compete fiercely but the CEOs are extremely competent and they all trust each other to be completely professional. I am biased when it comes to Latin America because I have great fondness for the region and I have very friendly relations with all of the CEOs. But I must say that some of the most enjoyable dinners have taken place in the region because of this special atmosphere, all wrapped up in a Latino flavour.

A leadership dilemma: colour and rules

Like the Latin American CEOs, I was also thinking of how to work around the constraints imposed by governments. I knew the industry could not be considered a normal business. Our profit margins make us look like a charity. And yet aviation is arguably one of the most important industries in the world, driving the global economy, connecting families and making the global village a reality. Normal businesses get to make and sell their product wherever it makes sense to do so. The components of a computer are manufactured in many different locations around the world and they are sold on a global basis. Governments have nothing to do. Airlines do not have this freedom. Governments limit market access and they constrain ownership. So I was constantly thinking about what IATA could do to update the colour of the balance sheet and the 60-year-old rules.

It was actually a controversial idea. Although it may seem that every airline would agree, in fact many relied on their governments for support. The government was their main or only shareholder and the rules it had put in place were keeping the airline alive. Many airlines were scared of transparency and a level playing field. I was convinced this couldn't continue. I wanted to put another "bomb in the church".

But it was difficult to find the right moment and the right way to address this critical issue. I knew from experience that you often only have one shot at a major issue and if you rush it you could lose everything and never get to present the idea again.

I decided the time was right at the Istanbul AGM in 2008. We had made a $5.6-billion profit in 2007, our first black number since 2000. Delivering a 1.1% margin while oil prices averaged $73/barrel was an amazing achievement. We had also secured a 10% reduction in charges at Seoul Incheon and got industry support for our Four Pillar environmental strategy. The star of the show, however, was e-ticketing.

We celebrated with a big applause and with confetti made from the last paper tickets floating down from the ceiling. We were the first industry in the world to go paperless, saving airlines $3 billion in the process.

But to get approval for my controversial idea, I needed to make the celebration short-lived.

The agenda for freedom

In my speech, after all these great results, I brought the AGM back to reality. I pointed out that 24 airlines had gone bust in the last six months because of the high price of oil and economic uncertainty. And it was possible that oil would continue to rise and average $135/barrel. That would put $99 billion on the industry fuel bill compared with 2007. I continued scaring the audience with numbers. Airlines had made $11 trillion in revenues over the last 60 years but had a profit of only $32 million. That's just a 0.3% profit margin. Airlines are near $200 billion in debt. I described aviation as being like Sisyphus—forever condemned to push a heavy weight uphill.

From a celebration the AGM atmosphere had become tense and worried. This complete switch in emotion gave me the opportunity I needed. I said it was time for the industry to be courageous and insist on change to the regulatory framework. I told the 1,000 participants that an Agenda for Freedom Summit that would focus on liberalizing the industry would take place in October 2008 in Istanbul. Leading countries, including the United States, Singapore and the United Arab Emirates, had already agreed to take part.

I had worked very hard to secure representation from these countries, using my personal relationships with Ministers of Transport and ICAO leaders. The Turkish Minister, Binali Yildirim, was a big help. He had opened our AGM in Istanbul and was very supportive of the industry.

He also had a great story to tell about how positive government policy could help turn around an airline's fortune. When I was CEO of Alitalia, Cem Kozlu was CEO of Turkish Airlines and he put in place the strategy that allowed the airline to flourish. Now under the leadership of Temel Kotil, the airline is one of the fastest growing in Europe.

Although we had a date and a venue for the Agenda for Freedom—to be exact it was the Ciragan Palace Hotel on the European shore of the Bosphorus—we had yet to decide on a Chairman. As is usual for these events, it had to be a respected global leader in his field. Fortunately, the choice was quite easy. Jeff Shane had worked for many years in the US Government as an Under-Secretary for Policy and was a respected Professor at Georgetown University. He had represented the United States at bilateral negotiations and chaired the 2007 ICAO Assembly. He has now joined IATA as its General Counsel.

At that first meeting in Istanbul I explained the situation and said we needed to equip airlines with the right tools to face crises in the future. I explained that my ten years at IATA had been dominated by colour and rules. The colour was red and the figures on the industry balance sheet always seemed to be in this colour. And the rules were 60 years old and needed to be retired.

There were ten countries in attendance and most of the representatives knew each other, so there was good chemistry from the start. Jeff was able to summarize and then settle the main points expertly. In the end, it was agreed that IATA would draft a statement outlining why governments should interpret bilateral agreements more liberally and that this statement would be endorsed by all the countries taking part.

Back in Geneva, Tom Windmuller and Carlos Grau Tanner, the IATA Director for Government Relations, began to work on a draft statement with Jeff Shane. They kept the ten countries updated and made sure nobody was left behind. I was busy trying to decide what my follow-up should be. Getting the European Commission on board seemed essential. I appreciated that it had a more difficult role because it had to represent all of its member states and there was still a divide between Northern and Southern carriers. My good relationship with EC Vice President Antonio Tajani was of great assistance. He was a clever and insightful business journalist in Italy before moving into politics, and in the end, I was able to get his full support. We all had to be very patient. I lost count of the number of drafts the Statement of Principles went through but every step was a step closer.

I was in constant touch with Roberto Kobeh at ICAO and also sought the wise advice of the former ICAO President, Dr Assad Kotaite. I also kept hammering home the message to governments that aviation is a vital part of the world economy and should be allowed normal commercial freedoms. I told them that liberalizing only 320 bilateral agreements would create 24.1 million jobs and add $490 billion to the global GDP.

A year after the first Summit there was a second meeting at Montebello in Canada, about 70 miles out from Montreal. Margaret Thatcher and Ronald Regan had once met here for a G7 Summit. Following two days of discussion we were able to agree and sign the statement. Chile, Malaysia, Panama, Switzerland, Singapore, United States of America, the United Arab Emirates all signed. The European Commission endorsed the statement and in the end we had some 60% of global aviation represented. Since then, the Statement of Principles has been endorsed by Bahrain, Kuwait, Lebanon and Qatar.

There are four main components of the Statement of Principles:

- *Freedom to access capital markets: states agreed not to exercise bilateral rights to block international services from airlines with non-national ownership structures.*
- *Freedom to do business: states agreed to focus on reducing restrictions on market access and to expedite further reopening of markets in future bilateral agreements.*

- *Freedom to price services: states agreed to focus on allowing greater freedom to price airline services in line with market realities.*
- *The need for a level playing field: states agreed that parties cannot be expected to implement these principles with governments that pursue policies designed to secure an uneven playing field for their national carriers, whether through restrictive practices, direct or indirect subsidies or other means.*

The US representatives, John Byerly and Paul Gretch, were instrumental in getting the project to a conclusion. I was also impressed with Aysha Al Hamili, a brilliant young pilot who represented the United Arab Emirates and later became one of the few women who have been on the ICAO Council.

It was an historic moment for the industry and an historic moment for IATA. Never before had a trade association been the driving force behind such an initiative. IATA had managed to get governments to agree. I worried at the beginning that they would think IATA was arrogant. But I was wrong and instead IATA came to be seen as a very positive voice for the industry.

A dramatic difference

The Latin America story and the Montebello initiative are two examples of airlines and IATA starting to think outside of the box. But far greater change is still needed if aviation is to have a sustainable future.

On the face of it, despite all the improvements that have been made, aviation's financial results are awful. During my ten years at IATA, airlines generated about $5.5 trillion in revenues. They ended up $20 billion down.

But there is a different story to tell. So much has been done that airlines can now break even with fuel at $110 a barrel. In 2002, when I started at IATA, the break-even figure was around $20. It is a dramatic difference built on greatly improved business processes and sophisticated technology. IATA certainly contributed to this success.

Another way of looking at this is how the various crises have affected the airlines. 9/11 cost airlines $21 billion and it took four years for them to recover the lost ground. The 2008 economic crisis cost airlines $94 billion and yet it took only a year to re-establish revenue levels. In 2010, the industry made a profit of $15.8 billion, a 2.9% margin, even as the global recession continued. This was so unexpected that some of my colleagues called for a celebration. I had many doubts about the message we would present though. Was a 2.9% profit margin really a cause for celebration?

I discussed the idea internally. We knew we would have a great location at the Berlin AGM in June 2010 in which to stage a celebration. The Gala dinner was due to take place at Templehof Airport, which had recently been decommissioned. It was built in 1927 and was once one of the largest buildings in the world. It's an impressive venue and would have been symbolic in the sense that aviation had outgrown it. But while it was tempting to at least acknowledge that the industry was moving in the right direction, the reality is that a single digit profit margin would get company CEOs in most other industries the sack. I couldn't bring myself to sanction anything that hinted of a slap on the back, a "Well done to us".

I began thinking that perhaps the best way forward was to look at how airlines could carry on making money into the future. Perhaps we could even identify how to improve the profit margin and make the industry truly sustainable? To do this, we would have to look back at what had gone wrong before and ahead to what we would do better in the future. The Vision 2050 project, as it became known, was born.

The think tank and the venue

We had a project but as yet no thoughts about who should be involved or the form it would take. To give weight to the enterprise, we needed to include respected airline CEOs as well as non-airline personnel. Manufacturers, airports, suppliers and even governments had to be included. I wanted a broad base of experience and skills as well as individuals with a global reputation. I was very happy that the likes of Ron Noble, Secretary General of INTERPOL, Nader Dahabi, former Prime Minister of Jordan and Anthony Albanese, Australian Minister for Infrastructure and Transport, agreed to take part.

We also needed everybody to meet, which meant we needed a venue. It had to be a country that had a government that supported aviation. That narrowed down the field quite considerably! The United States and Europe were definitely out. I briefly considered the three biggest emerging markets—India, China and Brazil. India was growing quickly but it was the size of the market that was impressive and not government policies. Although it had done well to open its skies, aviation in the country is still over-taxed. China is another market of huge potential but airlines there are still linked to the state, which wouldn't be appropriate for our Vision 2050. And Brazil was still struggling to get its infrastructure up to scratch even though it's got the World Cup and the Olympics coming up.

Chile was an interesting alternative. The merger of LAN and TAM, owned by the Cueto and Amaro families respectively, had created the second largest airline group by market value and the Chilean government is very supportive of aviation.

In the end, there was really only one option. Singapore is built on the efforts of its airline and airport. Aviation has been essential to the country's emergence since independence and under the guidance of Lee Kuan Yew aviation became a strong and competitive industry. In my speeches, I had often used Singapore as an example for other governments to follow.

Other governments had rarely had the courage to do so, of course, but that just made the promotion of Singapore all the more important.

Minister Mentor Lee closed the Vision 2050 conference with some fascinating insights into aviation and the role it had played as a pillar of the new Singapore state. Everybody present agreed afterwards: if only we had two or three more leaders with his vision and passion then our jobs in aviation would be made a lot easier.

With venue decided, the next step was to find someone to drive the meeting and subsequent report. It needed to be someone outside the industry. I didn't want Vision 2050 to be just another IATA document. The first ideas centred on the former political leaders, Bill Clinton and Tony Blair. A more academic study seemed appropriate, however. The industry needed to be analyzed and a clear path to profitability recommended. Airlines wanted to know how to make money.

It was Brian Pearce, the IATA Chief Economist, who came up with the idea of Michael Porter, a professor at the Harvard Business School and a world-respected expert on competitiveness. His book, *Competitive Strategy*, really changed the ways companies and governments viewed competition. So, Brian's suggestion made perfect sense to me and, as I was a member of the 1970 class at Harvard Business School, I was very pleased to welcome a colleague such as Michael to the project. I couldn't recall Michael though. I remembered many other professors—Hunt in Finance, Dearden in Accounting, Hesket in Marketing and Roland Christensen in Strategy—but I just couldn't place Michael.

Anyway, I asked Tom Windmuller, IATA's Corporate Secretary, to discuss our proposal with Michael Porter's team and keep me posted. It wasn't an easy arrangement because of the busy schedule of Professor Porter and because the study had to be ready well in advance of the Singapore meeting, which was scheduled for February 2011. Eventually, though, we managed to agree on the details of our cooperation and during one of my regular Montreal trips, I stopped in Boston to meet Professor Porter and explain the importance of Vision 2050 as well as express my appreciation for having him on board for this challenging project.

I've been back to Cambridge several times since I left Harvard. And every trip brings back memories of working in my small room at Cotting House, desperately studying for the next class. We used to debate solutions to particular business problems. Once in a while we got it right. But the best classes were the ones attended by a CEO who would follow our debate and then, at the end of the class, explain to us why our solution would never work in real life. You learn most from your mistakes. Certainly, my time at Harvard Business School has proved a real asset in my professional life.

At my meeting with Professor Porter I explained that we would need something available for the 2011 IATA AGM, which was also being held in Singapore. For his part, he was excited by the prospect of studying aviation, a sector he hadn't really touched on before. Having concluded our business, I asked what Professor Christensen was doing and Michael informed me that, sadly, he had passed away the year before. But when I mentioned Christensen he suddenly recalled bumping into me in the Professor's office all those years ago. Michael had been preparing his PhD while I was working on a book on my future employer, the Italian giant IRI. Memories came flooding back and we had a great conversation recalling our times as students together.

We didn't forget the work we had to do and at our meeting we agreed on monthly conference calls to discuss the latest updates on the project. It was on the second of these calls that Michael sighed deeply into the telephone. "Giovanni, I have never come across such a mess as aviation," he said. In a way, they were words of praise for airline CEOs. Michael meant that it was the industry structure that was wrong—all the uncoordinated, outdated regulations, the monopoly suppliers, the inability of airlines to act like a normal business. Airlines are in effect in a boxing match with one hand tied behind their back. They can never win.

Five Forces

The draft Vision 2050 document was sent to a 35-strong team we had assembled for the project in January 2011, a month before our scheduled Vision 2050 meeting. We needed to establish a roadmap for the industry, one they could use to guide them to a safe, green and profitable future.

The meeting was a great success and a very enjoyable experience. I think everybody learned something and that's the most you can hope for from a meeting of this nature. Michael Porter used his expertise and trademark "Five Forces" concept to explain the problem. Airlines have a perishable product with high fixed costs and any number of rivals. Customers and suppliers have all the power.

Michael's Five Forces framework starts with the **Intensity of Rivalry**. Needless to say, this is quite high in the airline sector. Several factors are behind this fierce competition. The product (the seat on an aircraft) is perishable and disappears whether it is used or not. Added to this, the product is very similar. Safety standards and aircraft design mean that differentiation is hard. Any innovation, such as a flat bed, is quickly copied. Price becomes the defining factor and so it gets ever lower. At the same time, fixed costs are high and getting higher. It is incredible to think that in 1945 it took the average Australian wage earner 130 weeks to pay for the lowest Sydney to London return fare. Now, they can do it in less than two weeks.

The second force is the **Threat of New Entrants**. This doesn't just mean new airlines but more usually existing airlines entering new markets. It should be seen in conjunction with the fact that there are high exit barriers in the industry. Normal returns in a sector rely on unsuccessful companies exiting the market, but in an average year, less than 1% of airlines disappear. Rules that limit foreign ownership and mergers are part of the problem. Alliances also play a part and can help partners through a lean period. And even if an airline disappears, its aircraft rarely do. Capacity stays in the market.

Michael then goes on to talk about the **Bargaining Power of Customers**. This is high and rising. Aggregator websites are concentrating this power for the individual while travel agents are responding to a more price-sensitive corporate market. Loyalty to specific airlines is low although there is some evidence that frequent-flyer programs are working.

Then there is the **Bargaining Power of Suppliers**. If we look at some key sectors in turn we can see the massive challenge faced by the airlines. Simply, there are not many airframe and engine manufacturers and so each has a strong market position. It's also worth noting that the defence sector is a big spender for these manufacturers, which further limits the power of commercial aviation. As for labour, I won't need to remind people who have been stranded on a bank holiday in Europe because of a French air traffic-controllers strike how powerful unions can be. Pilot unions across the world have often held an airline to ransom and cabin crew can also cause problems too, as British Airways and Finnair know only too well. I've spoken at length about airports in an earlier chapter, so I will just repeat that most are monopolies and their decisions about whether to expand or not are critical to airline success. It is also worth including sources of finance under this category. They are becoming rarer and those that still exist can push for far more attractive conditions than was previously the case.

The fifth and final force is the **Threat of Substitutes**. In Europe especially, high-speed rail is a serious competitor. It has taken a good share of the market on the heavy Madrid–Barcelona and Rome–Milan routes, for example. And we should also mention new communication technologies such as video conferencing, as these too have the power to dampen demand for air travel. But rather than other modes of transport and new technologies, the biggest substitute is the decision not to travel. It may be the cost, the hassle of security or the simple fact that the journey isn't essential.

Governments must listen

We realized early on that there was no silver bullet, no quick fix. But one thing is for certain. Governments must change. This isn't the same world as it was when the DC-3 was flying.

Much of this book has been critical of governments' aviation policies—with good reason. It is poor decision-making at the state level that has dogged this industry from the outset. If governments don't change their perception of aviation, the industry will continue to be held back. And when you think of the economic, social and cultural problems that will ensue, it seems clear to me that politicians must find some backbone.

First, they must agree to build new runways. Unless we get more runways, the system simply won't cope with the increase in traffic. What that means is that your young son or daughter won't be able to take the same flights or enjoy the same holidays and cultural exchanges that you do. It might mean they never get to see their grandparents or cousins who live in other countries.

Second, governments need to coordinate their security thinking into the Checkpoint of the Future concept. Nobody wants a repeat of 9/11 and nobody wants to wait more than 30 minutes in a queue and then have to undress and unpack.

Third, they must support biofuels. It is a young industry with huge amounts of promise. But it needs a kickstart—some supportive regulation that gives it a chance to establish itself. At the moment, there is no incentive for the big oil companies to change their ways and the cost of fuel is putting airlines under tremendous pressure. So governments must provide the carrot in some form of financial incentive to enter the industry and must then apply the stick with some hard targets and penalties for failure to comply. Biofuels will be a cornerstone of a sustainable aviation industry. I've mentioned how airlines can now break even at $110 a barrel. I wouldn't have thought that was possible so I may be wrong in suggesting that $150 a barrel is about the limit. We'll get to that price in the next few years. We've already seen peaks very close to that figure, so it's only a matter of time before we average it over a year.

Finally, governments must relax the rules to allow cross-border mergers. Airlines must have global access to financial markets. It will benefit the customer and the industry. Airlines are trying to serve modern markets with antiquated rules. It won't work. Financiers steer clear of aviation because of this. They know the industry is $200 billion in debt and has its hands tied. Airlines are not a good bet for investors.

Knowing what governments should do and actually getting them to do it are two very different things of course. But we cannot go on with regulation heaped upon regulation, tax heaped upon tax—it has to stop. Micromanagement of the industry just prevents normal commercial freedoms and distorts the market.

I believe governments are coming round to the industry point of view. I think the penny dropped when the volcanic eruption in Iceland stopped air travel in most of Europe. It cost the world GDP $5 billion, infuriated millions of passengers across the globe and stopped perishable goods getting to market. Farmers in Africa, from Kenya to Ghana to Zambia, suffered because of the eruption in Iceland. The World Bank put the losses for African countries at around $65 million.

Unfortunately, even if governments start making the right decisions straight away, it may already be too late. I suspect quite a few airlines will struggle in the years ahead and many will cease to exist. I support market forces and in a sense, a market correction like this may not be a bad thing. But the airlines will be killed off for the wrong reason. They should leave the market if they are weak or have been mismanaged and not because the governments have used them as a cash cow and milked them dry.

Serving the customer

The Vision 2050 project identified several other recommendations for a sustainable future. Anticipating customer needs is the start of the puzzle. Government knee-jerk reactions and a patchwork of regulations, infrastructure and technologies have left it near-impossible for an airline to provide the customer service they would want to provide. But, to be honest, if airlines had asked the question about customer needs 40 years ago, we may have seen a stronger industry. For years, airlines put unappetizing three-course meals in front of passengers when all they wanted was a cheaper flight.

This is what the low-cost carriers (LCCs) understood and why they have grown to be such a major force in the industry. In Europe, their market share has grown to near 40%. On the whole, LCCs have been a positive force in this industry. But these airlines too are having to adapt their business model for the modern customer and offer more services. AirAsia has shown that long-haul, low-cost travel is a possibility. But implementing AirAsia CEO Tony Fernandes' vision is not easy especially without a strong airline feeder system.

If we can win over the customer we will gain their support and then governments will have to listen to the industry. But serving the customer better will mean some difficult decisions. The ageing of the world population means many customers will be older. At the same time, there will be huge numbers of younger, technologically-savvy travellers. Flying will be second nature for these customers and they will have some very firm preferences.

For both sets of passengers, safety and security will remain the top priorities. There is every reason to believe that accidents will become increasingly rare, however, meaning that these priorities will not be reinforced too often. So passenger attention will turn to other areas.

Airlines will need to offer a range of products at a range of prices. Business travellers will want both speed and comfort and be prepared to pay for it. Older travellers will want comfort, too, but they're not in a great hurry and would prefer something a bit cheaper. Processes will have to account for their preferences at check-in and throughout the journey. The young will be very price-sensitive but they will want to be entertained and will expect to remain in constant contact with friends and families. These are generalizations though. Above all, the customer of 2050 will expect a travel experience tailored precisely to individual needs.

We need more runways

Processes have to be put in place that will deliver the desired experience. By 2050, the forecast is for 16 billion passengers a year compared with 2.9 billion today. Cargo will leap from 48 million metric tons to around 400 million metric tons. Although airlines are safer, leaner and greener than they have ever been, catering to those kinds of figures will necessarily involve some drastic changes in the business model and aviation processes.

Clearly, a large part of the problem will be physical. We'll need to develop airport terminals, increase airspace availability and, most importantly, build a lot more runways. In China, it won't be a problem. It is reported that there are plans for 56 new airports before the end of 2016. A further 16 airports will be relocated and 91 facilities will be expanded.

China's efforts are mirrored elsewhere in Asia. New airports there are constant award winners. But in Europe and the United States, infrastructure is a complicated issue to resolve. The "not-in-my-backyard" brigade is making it very difficult to build new runways. We won't get vertical lift-offs in the timeframe I'm talking about, so we have to find the land and the political will to build three kilometres of runway. It will be very difficult but there is the added benefit of connecting a city to the world rather than just another city. Try doing that with three kilometres of motorway or rail track. Unfortunately, politicians think short term. They want the votes that will win the next election and tend to push the harder decisions into the future. They must find the courage to explain to the younger generation that a sustainable aviation industry will be carbon neutral and is an environmentally-efficient mode of transportation.

The United Kingdom is always the obvious example in this regard. In 1971, the Roskill Commission debated London's aviation needs and a third runway for Heathrow. Some 40 years later and we're still talking about it. The number of destinations out of Heathrow has fallen, there are fewer connections to emerging markets like China compared with European rivals, and the airport is operating at over 99% capacity. London Heathrow used to suffer from more delays than the majority of its counterparts and only some good work from the air traffic authority, NATS, has prevented delays from increasing. Aviation in the United Kingdom supports 900,000 jobs and $81 billion in economic activity. The country is a cultural centre and British subjects are connected to work colleagues, families and friends throughout the world. The lack of a coherent aviation policy is astounding.

While the need for more runways won't change, airport design will be transformed. In my Vision 2050 initiative, experts such as Paul Griffiths, CEO of Dubai Airports, identified some interesting trends. In 2050, much of the administration of travel will take place prior to travel and behind the scenes. As mentioned in the previous chapter, the majority of passengers will simply walk through a security lane without stopping. Travellers will truly be able to relax and enjoy the airport experience. Designs will minimize distances to the aircraft gates and maximize amenity and retail space. People are already printing their own boarding pass and bag tags and this will become commonplace. The Vision 2050 report further suggests that Central Terminal concepts will disappear in favour of distinct concourses linked by train, which in turn connects with a high-speed system to the downtown area. Gate areas will change in conjunction with aircraft design. The main thrust will be to improve turnaround times, so getting passengers on and off the aircraft will be done as quickly as possible.

Once an aircraft gets in the air, it needs to fly in a straight line. The technology to do a green departure, optimize the trajectory and perform a continuous descent approach is available today. Only the political will to change is lacking. Like building runways, losing control of national airspace won't sit easy with governments, so I suspect that air traffic "management" rather than enablement will be around for some time yet.

Future technology

Fortunately, our technological capabilities are improving on an almost daily basis and that may give the industry some breathing space. Not all the technology necessary to serve the customer in 2050 is available today, but we're not too far off. Security is a good example. To make the Checkpoint of the Future a reality will take a machine capable of scanning a moving target. The best guess at the moment is that such a machine might be tested some time around 2014.

As for the aircraft themselves, they will be very different in 2050. When Kennedy told NASA to put a man on the moon within ten years, it had no idea about how to do that. And in 2008, when I said aviation had to be carbon-neutral from 2020 and produce just half the emissions in 2050 compared with 2005, I'm sure the aircraft manufacturers had no idea how that would be achieved either. But since then we have had winglets developed that reduce fuel burn a critical few percent. Once we get to blended wing designs, an incredible 32% improvement in fuel burn per seat is on offer according to the experts. There are all sorts of other ideas out there, from morphing wings to integrated engines. Who knows what else the engineers might come up with?

NASA has launched a project looking into advanced aircraft design. The goal is to get them to fly faster, further and carrying heavier payloads while burning a lot less fuel. There will be a lot of dead ends along the way but I'm sure we'll end up with designs that are a great improvement on the aircraft flying today.

Pretty much everybody that has made a prediction about technology has got it wrong, from the IBM chief who couldn't imagine why anybody would want a computer in their home to those who said that it was obvious that a heavier-than-air machine wouldn't fly. So I will not try and predict what technologies will be able to do for the airline industry in the future. But clearly the constant advances will make for a smoother travel experience and a safer travel experience.

On the fuel side, oil is only going to get more expensive. The need to develop biofuels is paramount and, as I explained in the environment chapter, it is a win–win scenario, able to develop jobs as well as reduce emissions. IATA supports the Solar Impulse project, an attempt to fly an aircraft around the world using only solar energy. The project's leaders are Bertrand Piccard and André Borschberg, who have often flown me in their hot air balloon high above the Swiss mountains. They deserve praise for their hard work and while we probably won't see commercial aircraft flying purely on the power of the sun, the invaluable data being gathered by the project will undoubtedly spark innovation among the major manufacturers.

Our greatest sin

It must also be admitted that the airlines themselves have to change. To serve the customer of the future airlines will have to be in business. Given the peanuts they have been earning so far, I'm not sure how many airlines around today will still be around in 2050. Airlines have to be sustainable. That means being green enough to have a license to grow and being profitable enough to give investors a fair return. There is about $650 billion tied up in the airlines, which should generate at least a $50-billion profit every year just to cover the cost of capital. After the $15.8 billion profit in 2010, a high for the 21st century, profits fell to just $8.4 billion in 2011, a 1.4% margin. Profit for 2013 is estimated at $10.6 billion (0.6%), a 1.6% margin. So even to get the cost of capital remains a dream.

Part of the problem is the value chain. Silos have to be broken down so that risk and reward are shared equally. An ultra-competitive sector such as the airlines cannot be held to ransom by monopolies further down the chain. But it is significant that when airlines cut capacity in the wake of the recent economic downturn the load factor—the average amount of seats sold—was 80.4%, the highest it has ever been. Airlines were helped by production problems at Boeing and Airbus and a rise in world trade, but major airlines had made independent decisions years earlier which resulted in constrained growth and capacity. And that gave the industry the $15.8 billion profit in 2010.

Recent experience of transatlantic markets has shown the importance of sensible capacity management. During the first half of 2012, US airlines faced a 2.5% fall in demand, due to the weakness of European economies and the sluggishness of the US economy. However, they cut capacity 4.9% and saw passenger yields improve 4.6%. US airlines have shown contrasting financial performance to other regions in the past 12 months with an improvement in cash flows and profitability, compared with deterioration for airlines in Europe.

It is a clear indication that capacity is aviation's "own goal", its greatest sin and a major key to long-term profitability. Keep the number of available seats down and airlines will make money. Increase capacity too much and the historical trend of a 0.1% profit margin will be as good as it gets. Unfortunately, IATA must remain silent about capacity and airlines must decide on capacity growth independently. What routes to fly and how often is a commercial decision and consequently very sensitive territory legally speaking. The competition authorities would have come down very heavily on IATA if they thought we were working in this area. Thanks to the support of my General Counsels, Bob McGeorge and Gary Doernhoefer—who both did an excellent job protecting IATA's legal interests—and some excellent training for IATA staff, IATA was never involved in any antitrust case.

But that left airlines to their own devices. For some, because of the flag on their tail, adding capacity is like adding prestige to their country. They start a new route not because they can make money but because it looks good to have a new connection with some distant capital. And they like the fact that their country's flag is visible at airports across the world. Others go for market share. Never mind the bottom line, just be the top dog in the market. The theory is that profits will flow in the long run, but it rarely works that way. Usually, bankruptcy comes first. Betting an airline's future on market share is never a good idea. All airline CEOs should abandon it.

What matters most in business is the figure at the bottom of the balance sheet. With airlines, we too often see that figure coloured in red. The problem with adding capacity is that it's very difficult to take away. What do you do with an aircraft you no longer need? You can't just put it on eBay. Airlines take a loss if they sell an aircraft in a downturn and getting rid of leasing contracts is equally costly. Keeping capacity avoids this capital loss. Remember too that you can't cut capacity by seat, you have to do it by aircraft. Changing to smaller aircraft simply increases the cost-per-available-seat kilometre. There are also slot rules at busy airports. If you don't use it, you lose it, which means airlines are tempted to keep aircraft flying. Finally, a CEO has to consider that cutting one flight might have a knock-on effect on the rest of the network. So, a route may no longer make money in itself but it could supply a number of passengers for a high-yield international service.

In short, it's much easier to add capacity than it is to reduce it. Even though the world is still in great economic difficulty, some 1,500 new aircraft were delivered in 2012.

Some airlines can hold off bankruptcy longer than others. When I was CEO of Alitalia most airlines were state-owned and there was a level playing field of sorts. But that isn't the case now. Private airlines have to fight against wealthy government-backed carriers. The Middle East carriers that are becoming so dominant refute that government backing is allowing them to add cheap capacity into markets for long-term gain, for example, but until they are quoted on international markets and publicly announce audit results, many will continue to believe that is exactly what is happening. IATA cannot say anything because it does not have an auditor role.

And while the Middle East may seem unique, every region has it opportunities and challenges.

Europe and the United States

One of the first things to recognize is that aviation's centre of gravity has shifted eastward. Europe and the United States were once leaders in the field. They were behind the Chicago Convention and its emphasis on safety has served the industry well. But when the Chicago Convention came into force, countries couldn't agree on the economic equation and so the bilateral system was born. It's a *quid pro quo* arrangement—one country's airlines can fly to destinations in another country so long as the favour is returned. Bilateral agreements worked okay when most airlines were state-owned. Prices were fixed at a small percentage above costs so every airline could make a bit of money and safety was never compromised.

But that was a long time ago now. Unfortunately, neither the United States nor Europe has shown the leadership needed to change the rules. I made a big effort in 2006 to get the ball rolling. The US Transportation Secretary, Mary Peters, and Vice President of the European Commission, Franco Frattini, two good politicians who looked to the future, worked alongside me to update the system. But James Oberstar, the strong Chairman of the House Transportation and Infrastructure Committee, was firmly opposed. Some in Europe were equally skeptical. We did eventually get the US–EU Open Skies Agreement in 2010, but this didn't go far enough and barriers to the foreign control of airlines still remain. You can get Campbell soups in approximately 120 countries, Google works in around 160 countries and IBM is present in about 170 countries. The airlines that have helped create the global village cannot enjoy this type of opportunity. The greatest reach of any airline has never reached three figures.

Airlines have done everything possible to work around the situation as mergers between Air France and KLM and Iberia and British Airways have shown. But it is still very difficult. In late 2012, Iberia announced plans to reduce its workforce by 4,000 people. Despite the good work done by Xavier de Irala with the support of the Spanish Prime Minister Jose Maria Aznar, the cost of the Spanish system and its ANSPs in particular is still too high. And the Chairman, Antonio Vasquez, has also been very effective. As a renowned tenor he can shout louder than most but the airline's pleas are still not being heard.

Airlines in the United States have also caught on to the potential of the merger. The United and Continental deal looks like being successful as it provides a strong domestic and international presence. The real surprise though was the US Airways and American Airlines $11-billion tie-up, announced in February 2013. Under the leadership of Bob Crandall, American had become an icon of the aviation community, but the company had been unable to re-engineer itself for the modern market. Doug Parker, the CEO of US Airways, will take charge of the new, merged airline and he will have to be fast in increasing market share in Asia, which is experiencing such a positive growth trend. It is worth mentioning that despite the consolidation taking place in the United States, fare increases have been limited to just 2% over the past decade. So consumers are still getting a great deal.

There are other bright spots in Europe and the United States. JetBlue, for example, is doing extremely well under the leadership of Dave Barger, who was able to solve the initial operational problems and create a very robust business model. Southwest, which has such a strong platform to build on thanks to the vision of Herb Kelleher, remains the biggest success story though.

But overall, Europe and the United States have become lost in the woods. The markets have matured and they are already being surpassed by other regions in terms of numbers and leadership. The Single European Sky and NextGen, for example, would bring so much in terms of the environment and efficiency, but they are just a 20-year-old dream. The politicians that led the way after the Second World War are gone and those in charge today haven't grasped that a modern industry cannot be held hostage to 60-year-old rules.

Asia-Pacific

Asia-Pacific is already the biggest aviation market in the world. And it's only going to get bigger. China is the standout country in this regard. I would have mentioned India, too, but it has been slipping recently as the government continues to heap taxes and enormous airport fees on airlines. The Air India–Indian Airlines merger has been very unsuccessful. I had supported Minister Patel opening up Indian skies and said that the best way to take advantage of all the new bilateral agreements was to have a strong Indian airline. But I warned him that any merger would need the full support of the government because it was liable to get very rough. Unfortunately, that has proved to be the case.

China has managed to maintain the momentum, however. It is not just about airline growth but also infrastructure growth. This has kept pace and created a virtuous circle, allowing airlines to grow. Even the consolidation of Chinese carriers happened within a couple of years when in the Western world it might have taken decades. The CEO of China Eastern, Liu Shaoyong, is an active member of the IATA Board and always made other members jealous when relating the speed of Chinese Government decisions and infrastructure implementation. China is also helped by the low cost of labour, of course, but it is the speed of decision-making that is the real advantage.

China has doubled its aircraft fleet in the past decade and it now has more international seats (1.4 million) per week than Japan. That would have been unthinkable ten years ago. In 2000, Japan had 480 aircraft and 1.2 million international seats every week. Twice that number was available on the domestic market. But Japan has stagnated and its experience shows that the region still needs to be monitored. To be fair, All Nippon Airways has always been at the frontline of efficiency as its decision to take the Boeing 787 shows. Under the leadership of Yoji Ohashi and then Shinichiro Ito, ANA took some important strides forward.

It should also be noted that Asia-Pacific isn't all about China. There are plenty of very interesting developments throughout the region. The turnaround of Garuda shows the work that has been done. Emir Satar, the CEO, was able to make a great turnaround in a short period starting from 2005. The airline has been profitable since 2007 and in 2011 issued an IPO.

Airlines' prospects could be helped by a new framework. ASEAN countries have agreed on a liberalization schedule and by 2015 it will be an open market. There is talk now of a Seamless Asian Sky and what's the betting that it will be in place before a Single European Sky? This kind of political will has been lacking in most other parts of the world. Combine it with the sheer numbers involved and Asia-Pacific has every reason to be cheerful about the future.

Achieving all that it has and with a strong future ahead, the region must accept some responsibility on behalf of the industry. It must be a leader in setting an agenda for the industry, helping to establish a framework that will facilitate a sustainable future. I feel sure that China will step up. We have already seen the major role it has played in underpinning the financial markets and it will do something similar in aviation, working carefully behind the scenes to make sure that this vital industry continues to bring benefits to the global village.

The Middle East

The region's overall market share has grown from 4% to 11% in the past ten years. Government and industry work well together. Taxes are low, the infrastructure is impressive and open skies agreements are always welcome.

But government and industry cooperation is also the problem. As noted above, the success of the Gulf carriers is treated with deep suspicion in the industry. Many believe it is government backing that is enabling the success of the airlines. This is very different from merely supporting the industry. Ensuring a level playing field won't be easy though. While it's true that airlines can fly into the likes of Dubai or Doha in return for Emirates or Qatar Airways getting access to their home markets, many do not consider this a fair deal.

The clearest example of this argument is the Air Canada–Emirates case. Air Canada successfully lobbied its government to stop Emirates increasing its flights to the country. Emirates say this is just denying Canadian citizens a great deal because they offer a superior product at a cheaper price. Air Canada, on the other hand, points to the implications for local jobs and the fact that getting access to Dubai is not the same as getting access to Canada. Apart from the size of the markets, Emiratis are far more likely to travel on their home airline than Canadians who are used to choice and have a cosmopolitan attitude to which airline they fly on.

The situation hasn't been helped by the global economic downturn, which is more deeply felt in the United States and Europe than it is in the Middle East.

So is there a solution? I'm not sure there's one that would be acceptable to all parties. One possible way forward could be to have airline balance sheets formally audited by respected international firms before traffic rights are granted. That would clear up some of the confusion and reveal if adding capacity to a market is justified or not. Whatever happens must be a business solution. It shouldn't be up to governments to sort this mess out. And airlines must resist the temptation to call on their governments as advocates or supporters.

The Etihad model of strategic codesharing partnerships and minority equity investments led by James Hogan also shows promise. Etihad has a very broad strategy and has shares in several other airlines, including airberlin, Virgin Australia and Air Seychelles. This may well be the best way forward for Gulf carriers and could start a consolidation process centred on the Gulf. Emirates, which came to prominence under the expert guidance of Maurice Flanagan, has always refused to enter an alliance and is usually quite reserved in these matters. But even Emirates has now signed a deal with Qantas to develop the so-called Kangaroo routes between Australasia and Europe. We may well see more of these deals in the future as it works well for all partners.

Africa

Africa remains a special case. Most of the airlines are struggling to survive, infrastructure is poor and safety is still an issue. There are exceptions but the continent as a whole continues to be a concern. Some countries are all but lawless and the authorities issue licenses to carriers without due regard for safety and it brings the entire region down.

The continent is divided by safety performance. Accidents for Western-built jets increased in 2012 to 3.71 (from 3.27 per million flights) and yet carriers on the IOSA registry are performing at or above average industry rates.

IATA, with ICAO and a host of other organizations, has committed to an Africa Strategic Improvement Action Plan aimed at addressing safety deficiencies and strengthening regulatory oversight in the region by 2015. The Plan was endorsed as part of the Abuja Declaration by the Ministerial meeting on Aviation Safety and Security of the African Union in July 2012.

Africa can get it right. The multi-state Agency for Aerial Navigation Safety in Africa and Madagascar (ASECNA), which was established in 1959 and provides air navigation services across a vast section of the African continent, is a great example of a coordinated approach. ASECNA recently froze charges for the eighth consecutive year.

And there are some great carriers too, worthy members of the world's major alliances. Kenya Airways' CEO Titus Naikuni has always been an active IATA Board member and his airline did a lot to help others through the Partnership for Safety. South African Airways gave IATA its first female Board member in Siza Mzimela. Egyptair and Ethiopian Airlines have also performed well under the circumstances. But none of these airlines can drag an entire region into the modern world.

Unfortunately, individual countries still do not understand the benefits that aviation can bring. Senegal has a $68 airport development fee. Several other countries such as Cameroon, Gambia, Mali, Niger and Sierra Leone also have high fees. This is not the way to encourage a sustainable industry in a region that desperately needs aviation for connectivity both internally and with the wider world. African aviation supports 6.7 million high-quality jobs and business activity totalling some $67.8 billion. The industry owes it to the continent to improve on this. With the right support from governments, it could play an even bigger role in facilitating Africa's growth and development.

Latin America

The traffic numbers aren't as impressive as Asia-Pacific but the aviation industry structure and the financial return certainly bear comparison. As in Asia, a number of airlines have developed supranational brands, getting round antiquated rules by setting up country-specific versions of the home airline. It's proved to be a good solution and airlines are posting profits consistently. The region is unique in that it has been profitable for four consecutive years. It's probably no coincidence that the region is connected to the world by airlines that have hit upon a business model that works around government regulations as I mentioned earlier.

Governments have played their part to a degree. Chile has a progressive aviation policy, for example. When you're stuck between the Andes in the East and the Pacific Ocean on the West, aviation becomes an important connector. During my last visit to the country as IATA Director General Emeritus in July 2011, I used the opportunity to present my successor, Tony Tyler, to the President, Sebastián Piñera. The President has had an extraordinary life and isn't a career politician. He graduated from Harvard Business School and as a successful businessman made his many millions through investments in television and airlines.

He has done an extraordinary job, though, rejuvenating the country after a devastating earthquake and managing the rescue of 33 miners, a story that gripped the world in 2010.

Following some impressive welcome protocols at the Palacio de La Moneda, including a formal military salute, we had a good meeting discussing aviation. President Piñera was kind enough to praise IATA for the work it had done in Latin American aviation. For Tony Tyler, it was the first example of the relevance IATA had managed to achieve over the previous decade. At the end of the meeting we were invited to take a walk through the Palacio de La Moneda. Built in 1805, it was originally a colonial mint and had been the centre of many upheavals in Chilean life, such as President Allende's suicide in 1973 following Pinochet's *coup d'etat*. I was reminded during the walk of a meeting Tony and I had in October 2009 at the Sheraton Hotel in Amsterdam when he was serving as IATA Chairman. We had to discuss the agenda for the next Board meeting and the succession process. He asked me about my retirement and I said that I would carry on until the June 2011 AGM, but that would definitely be it. "If I accept a year's extension the Succession Committee would have to find me a new wife, but I am very happily married," I joked. As we were talking, it occurred to me to say that Tony would make a really good candidate to be my successor. Two years later the Board agreed and Tony is doing a great job.

Even though Chile, and to a lesser extent the other Latin American governments, have put aviation on the national agenda, the really hard work has been done by the top managers at the airlines, who have shown determination and great vision to build a regional industry that has managed to be profitable for four years in a row. No other region can say that.

Aviation now supports in excess of four million jobs and more than $100 billion in economic activity in Latin America and the Caribbean. Those numbers will rocket. Chileans travel more than any other nationality in the region, but it is still just 0.7 trips per year. Americans, on average, travel 1.8 times a year.

There are still infrastructure and safety issues to address. Latin American airlines' safety improved in 2012 compared with 2011 (0.42 Western-built jet hull losses per million sectors in 2012 versus 1.28 in 2011), but the accident rate was still higher than the global average (0.20). As mentioned in Chapter 7, the IATA Operational Safety Audit will make the difference. The accident rate for non-IOSA carriers in the region is significantly worse than for those airlines that have met the standards. Chile, Brazil, Costa Rica, Mexico and Panama recognize this and have incorporated IOSA into their safety oversight. Peru is expected to follow in 2014.

Overall, the region has given itself a great platform on which to build.

The benefits of aviation

I've explained why airlines need a fair shot at success. They have a social and economic impact that should not be under-estimated. Let me put these arguments into figures. Globally, aviation supports near 57 million jobs and $2.2 trillion in economic activity. By 2030, these numbers will increase to 82 million jobs and $6.9 trillion in economic activity.

Where these increases occur is equally important. I have mentioned the importance of airlines to get African perishable goods to the markets in Europe. Many emerging countries rely heavily on the tourism sector too. Think of a safari holiday or a couple of weeks in a tropical paradise. It isn't possible to get to these places unless you fly. And unless tourists get to these places, the economies will stagnate because they rely heavily on the money that tourism brings. Think also of the Filipinos who work abroad and send money to their families, a practice that is vital to the Filipino economy and typical of many other countries.

We must not forget the role of aviation in day-to-day business. Air transport carries goods worth about $5.3 trillion every year. Some of these are critical, time-sensitive deliveries that only aviation makes possible, such as getting vaccines to distant markets. All of aviation is involved in humanitarian efforts. After the Haiti earthquake in 2010, British Airways flew two relief flights carrying Oxfam and UNICEF relief aid. Emirates donated several Boeing 747 freighter flights. Etihad, American Airlines and United Airlines also helped. Thai Airways flew 1,000 metric tons of rice donated by the Thai government. The famine declared in East Africa in July 2011 got a similar response. FedEx, UPS, Virgin and Lufthansa Cargo were among the many that rushed to help. It is not just about major disasters either. In October 2012, an Air Canada flight enroute to Sydney from Vancouver successfully located a yacht in distress off the Australian coast. An Air New Zealand flight coming into Sydney from Auckland was able to confirm the location and provide further details, enabling a successful rescue.

Aviation is a positive force in our global village. It makes possible the Olympics, the World Cup and the chance to see the incredible Terracotta Warriors in your home city. During my ten years at IATA we achieved many things, won many battles. But the fight to show that airlines are a force for good in this world goes on. I hope I have laid the groundwork for my colleagues in the industry to have a chance of winning that fight.

Airlines have been pushed around for too long.

Basta!

APPENDIX I

Industry figures 2001-11 (revenues, profits, fuel price, etc)

The following charts describe some of the major developments in global air transport markets over the past 40 years. They show an industry facing rapid growth in demand from travellers and shippers, but also vulnerability to extreme volatility and high fuel costs. Over this period it has not been possible for the industry to sustain more than minimal profits.

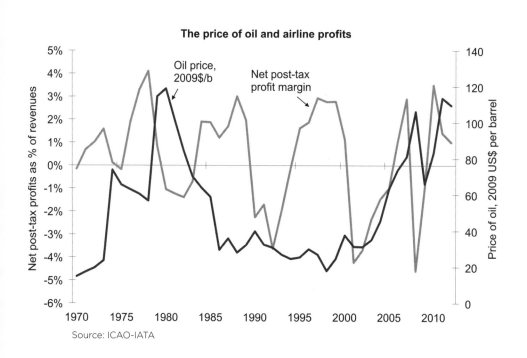

The price of oil and airline profits

Source: ICAO-IATA

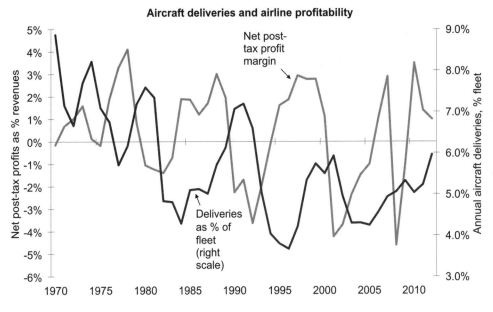

Aircraft deliveries and airline profitability

Source: ICAO-IATA

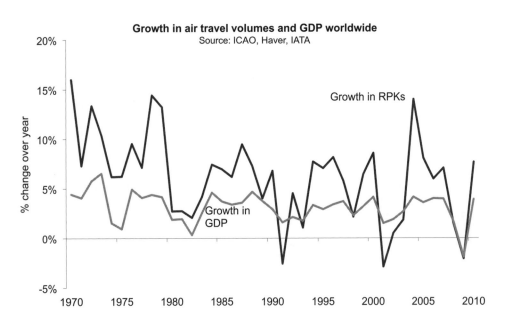

Growth in air travel volumes and GDP worldwide
Source: ICAO, Haver, IATA

Source: ICAO-IATA

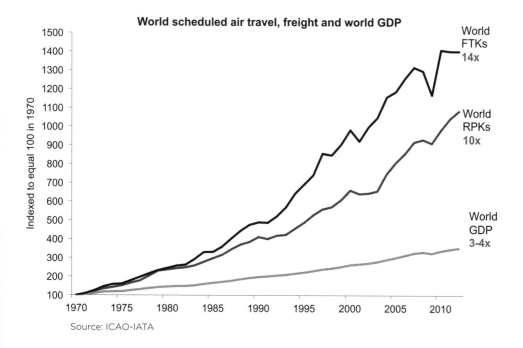

Source: ICAO-IATA

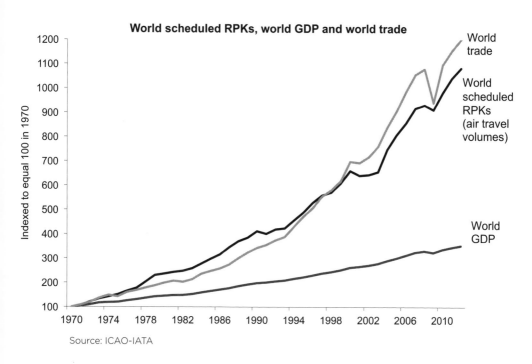

Source: ICAO-IATA

World scheduled freight volumes and world trade

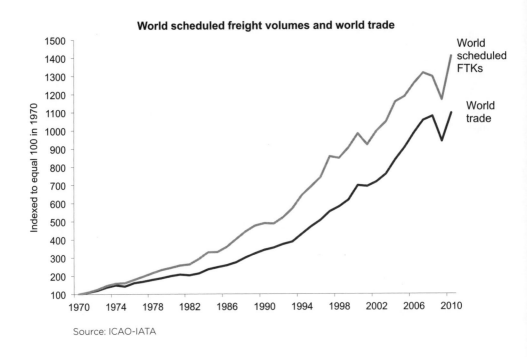

Source: ICAO-IATA

Utilization of passenger aircraft

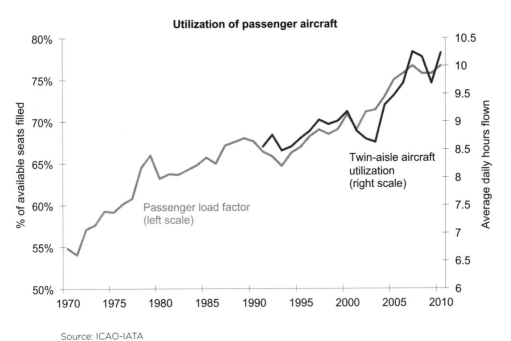

Source: ICAO-IATA

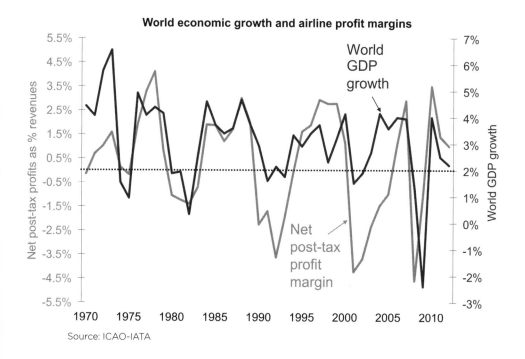

World economic growth and airline profit margins

Source: ICAO-IATA

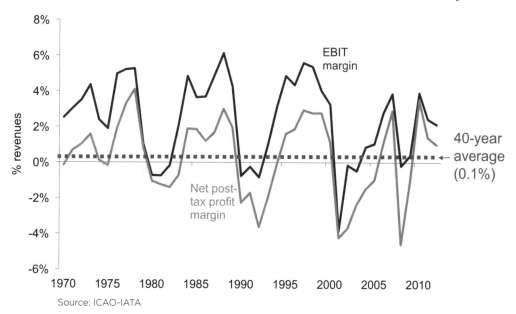

Profitability of the worldwide commercial airline industry

Source: ICAO-IATA

APPENDIX II

Extracts from Giovanni Bisignani's State of the Industry speeches, 2003-11

2003 59th AGM, Washington D.C

Summary: *A new, balanced approach to aviation; building a framework relevant to the reality of the day and ready for tomorrow's challenges; modernizing the three pillars of stagnation—bilateral agreements, ownership and competition.*

The three pillars of stagnation. Source: IATA.

Crisis is the only way to describe the state of our industry today. IATA members lost $3.8 billion on their international services in 2002. That makes over $14 billion dollars in two years. And when we include domestic losses, globally the industry lost almost $25 billion in 2001 and 2002.

Our industry has been hit by the Four Horsemen of the Apocalypse. The successive impact of September 11, a world economic slowdown, Iraq and SARS has been devastating. Our industry was like the boxer who gets hit harder after every knockdown! But under tremendous pressure, our industry has also shown the ability to change. And change dramatically.

The challenges are many. To address them we need speed, passion, commitment, knowledge and leadership. IATA, as the voice of our industry, must communicate strongly and effectively. I also see IATA as an agent of change. Because change is what our industry needs the most.

2004 60th AGM, Singapore

Summary: *Remaining vigilant on costs and collectively supporting the drive for change; not stopping until the last barrier to change disappears; getting governments to demonstrate leadership for the future, not defence of the status quo.*

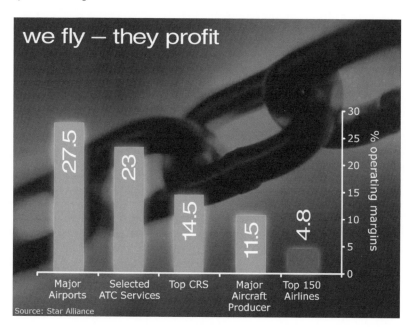

Some challenges—like the high price of fuel—are universal. Our projections of a $3-billion dollar profit this year were based on an average oil price of $30. If oil prices average $33, we break even. At $36 we could expect $3-billion losses.

Your association has been at your side, fighting the many fires that have affected the industry. Last year we achieved $63-million cost savings from airports and air navigation service providers. This year, airports from Vienna to Seoul reduced or rolled-back increases in user charges. We shouted in a polite way when Toronto gave our industry a Versailles with boarding bridges.

The industry will not pay for extravagance. I will continue to be a thorn in the side of partners who do not understand our needs. Our protests eliminated cross-subsidy in privatization plans for Narita. In Hong Kong, IATA engaged the government to ensure that economic regulation was included in airport privatization plans.

The message must be clear: air transport is the economic lifeblood of a community. Governments must stop milking the industry to solve their inefficiencies or a city's budget problems.

We are taking the European Union to court to fight misguided regulations concerning compensation for flight cancellations and delays. They wanted to make airlines take responsibility for snow! It is high time that European Union regulators took the trouble to learn about the industry they are busy mis-regulating. Our achievements helped the industry survive three very difficult years. Now, we must move from fighting fires to designing new industry structures.

Consumers pay for value, not for complexity. The traditional model is being pressured in all corners of the globe. The challenge is to retain the value of the network system but eliminate the costs of complexity. Our future structure is a low-cost industry, with some airlines offering network services at a premium the consumer is willing to pay for. We must shift our agenda from fire-fighting to building a new industry structure. The key new design element is Simplifying the Business. To move forward, we need strong leadership and a vision of change that is shared by all stakeholders.

2005 61st AGM, Tokyo

Summary: A five-point agenda for change:

- *Governments must stop treating us like cash cows.*
- *Governments must ensure that monopoly providers get serious about cost efficiency.*
- *Governments must stop distorting competition.*
- *Governments must stop micro-managing the industry.*
- *Give us the freedom to run our business like any other business.*

Source: IATA

My concern is the bottom line. Losses between 2001 and 2004 exceeded $36 billion. And we will lose another $6 billion in 2005. Parts of the industry are profitable. But the margins are not acceptable for a $400-billion industry. Urgent action and change are needed.

Your association is changing as well. Some 60% of our team is new.

And we are 14% leaner. We have new expertise and a new culture. Your priorities are now our top priorities. Our obsession with efficiency has driven costs down. Cost-cutting allowed us to return $6 million to airlines in our settlement systems. We are investing $11 million in industry projects like safety and Simplifying the Business alone. This is $17 million. This is more than we collect in dues.

More importantly, this year we expect to save the industry at least $1 billion in taxes, charges and fees; and $700 million in route improvements.

We have one great advantage. We have a clear vision and we are passionate about our future. A future as

- *A low cost, environmentally responsible industry*
- *that safely and securely connects the globe*
- *provides value to passengers and shippers*
- *and supports global economic development.*

2006 62nd AGM, Paris

Summary: *Sending out wake-up calls; airlines must keep focused on efficiency; unions must understand that to share in success means being part of the solution; Global Distribution Systems must deliver value for money; fuel suppliers must realize that profiting without investing is not acceptable; airports must appreciate that efficiency is coming; and governments must not kill us with an overdose of taxation.*

Government wake-up call:

Don't kill us with an overdose of tax

Source: IATA

We are starting to see light at the end of a five-year tunnel—some cautious optimism.

Since 2001 labour productivity improved 33%, sales and distribution costs dropped by 10%, and overall non-fuel unit costs reduced by 13%. Airline efforts have moved the break-even fuel price from $14 per barrel to $50. We are en-route to a low-cost industry. We have not yet landed—but the approach is near.

Facts and figures highlight our responsible approach to our most important issues. But too often stakeholders, who lack the vision and speed to match our achievements, block our progress.

Our customers should be angry. Your choice is restricted by an outdated bilateral system. Your cheap tickets are expensive because politicians add taxes. Your time is wasted because governments cannot organize direct, environmentally friendly routes. Your money subsidizes airport inefficiency because governments have failed to regulate monopolies. And you wait too long for shipments to arrive because governments are not living in the Internet world.

2007 63rd AGM, Vancouver

Summary: *Air transport must become an industry that does not pollute; the potential building blocks for a carbon-free future are already in place.*

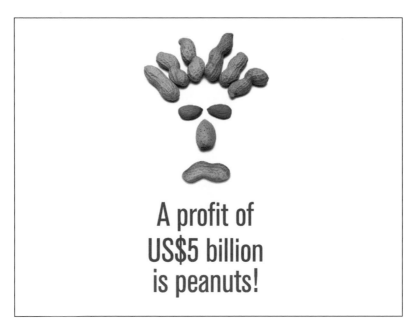

A profit of
US$5 billion
is peanuts!

Source: IATA

We are now a $470-billion industry and a profit of $5 billion is peanuts. We need $40 billion just to cover the cost of capital. We are moving in the right direction but the financial hole is deep. The industry is $200 billion in debt. Our financial foundation is weak.

Another challenge is coming into view, the environment. Our track record is good, reducing noise 75% and improving fuel efficiency 70%. The billions being invested in new aircraft will make airlines a further 25% more fuel-efficient by 2020. So even as demand for travel increases, the increase in our carbon footprint will be limited. The UN estimates that we will grow from 2% of total carbon emissions to just 3% by 2050.

But we have been silent in our success and now we have a reputation crisis. That makes us an easy target for politicians who think green and see cash. Despite a good track record and a strong policy, we have been weak communicators. So we are working with you and our industry partners to raise the volume of our communications. But this is only part of the solution.

Our carbon footprint is growing and that is not politically acceptable—for any industry. Climate change will limit our future until we change our approach from technical to strategic. Strategy starts with vision: for Toyota, it's an Earth Charter, GE has ecomagination and BP has Beyond Petroleum. So what is our vision?

Let me start the debate by aiming high. Air transport must become an industry that does not pollute. Zero emissions. I don't have all the answers but our industry started with a vision that we could fly. The Wright Brothers turned that dream into reality and look at where we are now. We can see potential building blocks for a carbon-free future.

2008 64th AGM, Istanbul

Summary: Giving every airline the commercial tools to manage crises effectively and the opportunity to compete globally on a level playing field; urgent action is needed to communicate clearly to governments the dimension of the crisis, the potential impact on the global industry if our industry fails, the measures airlines are taking and the action that they must take; an Agenda for Freedom Summit will help to drive much bigger change that will free airlines from national flags, secure financial stability and create global opportunities.

Source: IATA

Our industry is like Sisyphus. After a long uphill journey, a giant boulder of bad news is driving us back down.

It's another perfect storm. The spreading impact of the US credit crunch is slowing traffic growth. At best we expect 3.9% this year. After enormous efficiency gains since 2001 there is no fat left and skyrocketing oil prices are changing everything. For every dollar the price of oil goes up, costs go up by $1.6 billion. If oil stays at $135 for the rest of the year, losses will be $6.1 billion. The situation is desperate and potentially more destructive than our recent battles with all the Horsemen of the Apocalypse combined.

The crisis is also a catalyst for governments to deliver results on the environment that reduce fuel burn. Even before the fuel crisis our vision to address climate change set the benchmark for all industries—carbon-neutral growth, leading to a carbon-free future. IATA's Four Pillar strategy is driving progress to deliver real reductions in CO_2, by investing in technology, flying planes effectively, building efficient infrastructure and implementing positive economic measures. Our attention to the environment also includes the little things. This is our first carbon-neutral AGM.

Crises are opportunities to drive bold changes. Four years ago in the wake of a crisis we had a vision to modernize our business with technology, improve convenience and save $6.5 billion. Today that vision is a reality. The star of the show is e-ticketing. Together we made 100% e-ticketing a reality. Congratulations. Thanks to all of you, a great industry team, and for a great industry effort. Working together we achieved enormous change.

2009 65th AGM, Kuala Lumpur

Summary: *The biggest job is resizing and reshaping the relationship with governments; climate change is a priority but moving from punitive taxation to joint problem-solving is also vital.*

If governments are too slow to invest they are too fast to tax

Source: IATA

How long must we travel the desert of global recession? There is no modern precedent for today's economic meltdown. Cargo remains a good leading indicator. Its 23% freefall in December was a clear sign that the global economy was collapsing. It has been stable at that level for five months.

This may be the bottom but recovery is different. Banks are still not able to finance business. $1 trillion is still needed to re-capitalize. Our customers don't have confidence. They need to reduce debt and that means less cash to spend. Business habits are changing and corporate travel budgets have been slashed. Video conferencing is now a stronger competitor.

Our relationship with governments must move from punitive micro-regulation to joint problem-solving. Governments must understand that we can help them protect their citizens, improve efficiency, save jobs and support economic growth, but only if we work together.

Let me be clear. We don't want bailouts. All we want is access to global capital, but old rules stand in the way of a healthier industry. If we cannot pay the bills, saving the flag on the tail will not save jobs. A prolonged recession could lead to a cash crisis. This would put at risk 32 million jobs and the lifeblood of the global economy.

2010 66th AGM, Berlin

Summary: *The industry needs to have a vision for the future; how can it get to $100 billion in profits on revenues of $1 trillion?*

Source: IATA

The last decade tells us that this industry is capable of enormous change. We cut the accident rate by more than one-third. We survived the spike in oil prices to $144 a barrel. We improved labour productivity by 63%. Alliances grew from infancy to 56% of traffic. We developed Asia-Pacific into our largest market, one-third of all aviation. We found a global solution on noise and we are now focusing on carbon emissions. Your association worked with you to drive change with speed. Since 2004, we saved 70 million metric tons of CO_2. In 48 months, we delivered e-ticketing 100% in every corner of the planet. Working together over the last six years with programs led by your association, we saved the industry over $47 billion. The progress of our industry through your hard work has been amazing.

But today's industry structure will not deliver the profits we need. In a decade when airlines lost $5 billion a year, 574 airlines started operations and less than 200 disappeared. Barriers to exit are too high and barriers to entry are low. With 1,061 airlines, we are the world's most fragmented industry. Even with the recent round of mergers, the top 20 carriers only account for half the global industry. Efficiency gains never make it to the bottom line because we are deprived of the commercial freedom to operate like a normal business. And poor profitability makes every shock a fight for survival. The restrictions of the bilateral system are a dam that holds us back. It's time for that dam to burst.

I see a future where governments act responsibly, ensuring safety, security and a level playing field. A future where airlines can build efficiencies across borders to better serve their customers, and achieve sustainable profits to fund growth and innovation.

2011 67th AGM, Singapore

Summary: *Airlines spent a decade in survival but IATA supported every airline, big and small; it is important to maintain the momentum for change and Vision 2050 will provide a framework.*

Don't kill the goose that lays the golden eggs

Source: IATA

Terrorism, wars and revolutions. Pandemic fears, earthquakes and volcanoes. Failing economies and skyrocketing fuel prices. Over the last decade we have seen everything. Everything, except sustainable profits.

Airlines spent a decade in survival mode. Change was harsh. Hundreds of thousands of jobs disappeared, and we said goodbye to many famous companies—Swissair, Varig, Ansett, Sabena, Mexicana and Aloha.

In the aftermath of 9/11, IATA took on the role of fireman, responding to emergencies. IATA led with speed, passion and commitment. We started with monopoly suppliers. Living in a different reality, they offset declining demand by increasing prices. Shouting politely, we instilled a new mindset that saved airlines $17 billion in costs for airports, air navigation service providers and fuel suppliers.

IATA's role quickly changed to architect, because the industry needed a radical redesign.

IATA had to support all its members, not just the club of the powerful. Every airline—big and small—had to share the benefits. To succeed, we set targets. This was unthinkable for an association, but IATA provided support and you delivered.

Innovation and openness to change will determine our future. The changes of the last decade prove that we are capable. Airlines, governments and even your association will be challenged to adapt to new business and demographic realities. We need to keep this momentum, to drive change everywhere, not as a response to crisis, but as a way of doing daily business.

The challenge for my successor is to increase relevance by driving even more change; to keep the industry united, bridging differences and building on our many great successes; and to keep IATA focused as a global association that represents, leads and serves all of its members equally.

My confidence in the future reflects the great people who manage and lead our industry. Let me thank the ICAO leadership for solid partners; my four predecessors who built IATA's foundations; my great IATA team who supported me on this wonderful journey; and finally the Board, our member airlines and those partners and governments which embraced change.

Thank you for trusting my leadership and supporting my many crazy ideas.

APPENDIX III
Table of people

Chapter 8: BAD PEOPLE, NOT BAD OBJECTS
The need for more efficient and harmonized security

A knee-jerk reaction

Admirals in the air
Tom Ridge, Michael Chertoff, Bernie Korkik, Admiral Loy, Admiral Stone, Franco Frattini, Janet Napolitano

The Amsterdam incident
Janet Napolitano, Silvia Krahl

Trusting the shipper

Security costs

Tomorrow's system today
Ken Dunlap, Janet Napolitano

Chapter 9: VISION 2050
A look at Vision 2050, liberalization and thoughts on the future

The need for change

The Latin American model
Cristina Fernández, Patricio Sepulveda, Mariano Recalde
Fernando Pinto, Ozires Silva, Omar Carneiro Da Cunha, Enzo,
Germán Efromovich, Juan Cueto, Enrique Cueto, Ignacio Cueto,
Rolim Amaro,

A leadership dilemma: colour and rules

Agenda for freedom
Binali Yildirm, Cem Kozlu, Temel Kotil, Jeff Shane
Tom Windmuller, Carlos Grau Taner, Antonio Tajani, Assad Kotaite
John Byerly, Paul Gretch, Aysha Al Hamili

A dramatic difference

The think tank and the venue
Ron Noble, Nader Dahabi, Anthony Albanese
Lee Kuan Yew, Cueto and Amaro families
Brian Pearce, Michael Porter, Harvard Professors
Michael Porter

ABOUT THE AUTHOR

Giovanni Bisignani is a member of the Board of NATS Holdings Limited, the UK's air traffic services provider. He is also a member of the Board and Strategic, Remunerations and Nominating committees of SAFRAN Group, a holding company which encompasses aircraft engine manufacturing, aerospace, defence and security activities, partially owned by the French Government. He is a member of the Board of AirCastle (US), a global aircraft leasing company, and of the World Economic Forum Global Agenda Council on Aviation, Travel & Tourism (Switzerland). He is a Visiting Professor at Cranfield University–School of Engineering (UK).

Giovanni was Director General of the International Air Transport Association from June 2002 to July 2011. He became Director General Emeritus from June 2011 until his retirement in October 2011. During his nearly ten years with the organization, Giovanni drove major industry changes. The most important was making the IATA Operational Safety Audit (IOSA) a condition of IATA membership. This contributed to a 58% improvement in safety over the period 2002-11.

Giovanni also started the Simplifying the Business (StB) initiative in 2004. During his tenure, this program converted the industry to e-ticketing and bar-coded boarding passes, made common-use self-service kiosks as an integral part of the travel experience and established the framework for 100% e-freight by 2015.

Giovanni mobilized the industry behind an ambitious strategy to deal with the impact of the industry's carbon emissions on climate change. Airlines, airports, air navigation service providers and manufacturers committed to achieve carbon-neutral growth by 2020 and cut emissions in half by 2050.

Finally, Giovanni strengthened IATA's financial clearing systems, which processed US$ 2.5 trillion during his mandate. He was also the strong voice of IATA, firmly lobbying governments to focus on long-term issues affecting the viability of aviation. He was particularly outspoken on liberalization, taxation and environment.

Giovanni's career prior to joining IATA spans several industries. In 2001, he launched the European travel portal OPODO and spent five years as CEO and Managing Director of Alitalia during 1989–94. During this time he also served on the IATA Board of Governors and was Chairman of the Association of European Airlines (AEA) in 1991. He was a member of the Pratt & Whitney Advisory Board and Chairman of Galileo International UK and Covia US (1993–94), leading companies in the global travel distribution system industry. He also held directorships at Finsider, Fincantieri, Italstat, Sme, Assolombarda and was Chairman of Merzario USA (1998–2001). Giovanni began his career in New York with the First National Citibank and then held several high-level positions at the energy company ENI and with the Italian industrial conglomerate IRI Group. From 1994 to 1998, he served as President of Tirrenia di Navigazione, the largest Italian ferry company and, from 1998 to 2001, as CEO & Managing Director of SM Logistics, a group of logistics and freight forwarding companies partially owned by GE.

Giovanni studied both in Italy (Università La Sapienza – Economic & Commerce School) and the United States (Harvard Business School). In June 2008, he received the honorary degree "Doctor of Science honoris causa" from the School of Engineering at Cranfield University in the United Kingdom, becoming a Fellow of the Royal Aeronautical Society the following year. Born in Rome in 1946, he speaks Italian, English and Spanish. He is married with one daughter and enjoys golf, tennis and riding.

GOLD MERCURY
INTERNATIONAL
Sustainable vision for a complex world